GRE
Mathematics
Subject Test
Solutions

Exams GR1268, GR0568, and GR9768

3rd edition

CHARLES RAMBO

Contents

Preface

Thank you for checking out my GRE mathematics subject test solutions for exams GR1268, GR0568, and GR9768. It was a pleasure to write this booklet, and I hope you find the solutions to be a valuable resource.

The purpose of this text is simple: It's to help students study. This booklet is intended to have enough detail to help struggling students understand key concepts. The design is such that solutions are self-contained and you can easily see what theorems are used. Major theorems are precisely formulated, either within the main text, the glossary, or both. In particular, theorems from lower-division mathematics courses are cited frequently, because it has probably been a long time for most of you. Everything is written from an intuitive perspective, and very few proofs are contained within the text.

My apologies for any errors. Alas, one of the problems with self-published material is that it's not always feasible to hire editors. And I must admit that I'm not the most careful writer. I welcome your help: If you find errors or have questions please feel free to email me at `charles.tutoring@gmail.com`. Past feedback has really improved the solutions. In particular, you guys found about a dozen errors in the text, which have all been fixed so they won't confuse future readers. Keep it coming! It has been a pleasure to hear from you all.

A plethora of resources was utilized while crafting this booklet, and I would like to explicitly acknowledge a subset of them. Obviously, the exam questions on which these solutions are based were written by *Educational Testing Service*; you can view the original exams at `rambotutoring.com/math-gre/`. *Wikipedia* was extensively used for theorems; sometimes whole theorems were simply copied and pasted into this document with only minor changes. When this was done, a link in the glossary to the original theorem was included. Rudin's *Principles of Mathematical Analysis*, Stewart's *Calculus*, *Schaum's Outline of Discrete Mathematics* by Lipschutz and Lipson, and *Counterexamples in Analysis* by Gelbaum and Olmsted were all invaluable resources, and I recommend them to you. It was also helpful to look at solutions posted on the *Math Stack Exchange* and *MathematicsGRE.com*. And the *LaTeX Stack Exchange* was of great utility to me for information about LaTeX.

I would like to thank the artist that created this booklet's lovely custom cover. They put a lot of time and effort into this project, and for that I am greatly appreciative. I wish my words were enough to express my gratitude. They requested not to be identified by name. However, you can view their website at `skraps.xyz`.

While preparing for the math GRE, I recommend old exams as your first resources. Past performance is the best indicator of future performance, so try your best to take old tests using actual exam conditions. In particular, be mindful of the time constraint, because it makes the exam substantially more difficult. Each test has 66 questions and you'll have 170 minutes to complete them, which means you have about two and a half minutes per problem. The techniques used here should be viable given those time constraints. However, no one is more qualified than you to optimize your time management system. You want to know how long it takes you to complete mathematical tasks with accuracy, when it would be best to skip or give up on a problem, and when it's best to push through and get one done. Please keep this in mind as you read the solutions, and frequently time yourself as you work through problems.

Your solutions will not require proofs, and it's not necessary to show a lot of detail. In this sense, most solutions here do not mimic how one ought to solve problems during the exam. The reason for this is because this text is intended to be both didactic and a reintroduction to concepts from lower-division courses.

If you're in need of further GRE preparation material, there are a few other resources available. Of course, I would like to recommend my own book, *Practice for the GRE Math Subject Test: One Practice Test and Solutions*. It contains one practice test, solutions, and a glossary much like the one here. The book *Cracking the GRE Mathematics Subject Test* is also good. Its questions are very similar to those on the GRE, and it has very well done chapters that explain what you need to know and each one contains a little mini-test at the end to assess your understanding. But *Cracking the GRE Mathematics Subject Test* does have some issues; problems are a little easier than would be ideal and there are a lot of mistakes. The REA book *GRE Mathematics* is helpful too, mainly due to its difficulty, but the authors weren't able to emulate the actual math GRE test closely. My website `rambotutoring.com/math-gre` has a whole bunch of other math GRE content as well.

Lastly, at the risk of sounding patronizing, I hope you enjoy studying for the GRE. Taking a standardized test is a high-pressure ordeal, and students are often preoccupied with what comes after the test. But the problems tend to be well done, and questions are designed to be more about finding clever approaches than about relying heavily on memorization or computation. That's a good thing. And as a general tip, life is more enjoyable if you take the time to appreciate the things you're doing in the moment.

Good luck on the GRE!

Charles Rambo

Escondido, California
January 2018

Chapter 1

GR1268 Solutions

Question 1.1. ─────────────────────────

When we plug 0 into the expression for x, we obtain the ratio $0/0$ which is an indeterminate form. According to *L'Hôspital's rule*, when a ratio is in the $0/0$ indeterminate form, the limit is equal to the limit of the ratio of the derivatives of the top and bottom. So,

$$\lim_{x \to 0} \frac{\cos(3x) - 1}{x^2} \overset{LH}{=} \lim_{x \to 0} \frac{-3\sin(3x)}{2x}$$

Notice that the new limit is also in the $0/0$ indeterminate form, which means that we can apply L'Hôspital's rule again:

$$\lim_{x \to 0} \frac{-3\sin(3x)}{2x} \overset{LH}{=} \lim_{x \to 0} \frac{-9\cos(3x)}{2}$$
$$= \frac{-9\cos(0)}{2}$$
$$= -\frac{9}{2}.$$

Hence, we select (E). See *sine and cosine values in quadrant I* in the glossary for a table of sine and cosine values at popular radian measures. ∎

Question 1.2. ───────────────────────────────

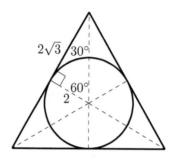

Since the circle is inscribed within an equilateral triangle, it is tangent to the triangle at all points of intersection. This implies that the radius of the circle is perpendicular to the triangle at intersection points. With this in mind, we divide the equilateral triangle into six congruent right triangles.

Each of the right triangles is a $30° - 60° - 90°$ special right triangle. This is because the hypotenuse of each right triangle bisects an interior angle of the equilateral triangle. As a result, one interior angle of each right triangle must have measure $60°/2 = 30°$, which implies the other acute angle has measure $90° - 30° = 60°$.

We will find the area of each of our right triangles. Let the radial length of 2 be the length of each triangle's height. Then the base of each right triangle has length

$$2\tan(60°) = 2\sqrt{3}.$$

Hence, each right triangle has area

$$\frac{2(2\sqrt{3})}{2} = 2\sqrt{3}.$$

Because all six right triangles are congruent, the total area of the equilateral triangle is

$$6(2\sqrt{3}) = 12\sqrt{3}.$$

The correct answer must be (C). ■

Question 1.3. ———————————————————

Let $u = \log x$, which implies $du = dx/x$. Hence,

$$\int_{e^{-3}}^{e^{-2}} \frac{1}{x \log x}\, dx = \int_{x=e^{-3}}^{e^{-2}} \frac{du}{u}$$

$$= \int_{u=\log e^{-3}}^{\log e^{-2}} \frac{du}{u}$$

$$= \int_{-3}^{-2} \frac{du}{u}$$

$$= \log |u| \Big|_{-3}^{-2}$$

$$= \log 2 - \log 3$$

$$= \log \frac{2}{3}.$$

We conclude that the answer is (D). A list of *logarithm properties* is located in the glossary. ∎

Question 1.4. ———————————————————

This reduces to an equivalent problem with *bases*, since every subspace has a basis and the number of elements in a basis is its dimension. Consider a basis for $V \cap W$ and extend it to a basis of V. Let the set $\mathcal{B}_1$ be this basis for V. Extend $\mathcal{B}_1 \cap W$ to a basis of W, and call it $\mathcal{B}_2$. Extend $\mathcal{B}_1 \cup \mathcal{B}_2$ to a basis of X, and call it $\mathcal{B}$. We need to find what the cardinality of $\mathcal{B}_1 \cap \mathcal{B}_2$ cannot be. Using the *inclusion-exclusion principle* on $\mathcal{B}_1$ and $\mathcal{B}_2$,

$$|\mathcal{B}_1 \cup \mathcal{B}_2| = |\mathcal{B}_1| + |\mathcal{B}_2| - |\mathcal{B}_1 \cap \mathcal{B}_2|.$$

Since $\mathcal{B}_1 \cup \mathcal{B}_2 \subseteq \mathcal{B}$,

$$|\mathcal{B}_1| + |\mathcal{B}_2| - |\mathcal{B}_1 \cap \mathcal{B}_2| \le |\mathcal{B}|.$$

Because $\dim(V) = \dim(W) = 4$ and $\dim(X) = 7$, we have

$$4 + 4 - |\mathcal{B}_1 \cap \mathcal{B}_2| \le 7 \quad \text{implies} \quad |\mathcal{B}_1 \cap \mathcal{B}_2| \ge 1.$$

Therefore, $V \cap W$ cannot have dimension 0, and we pick (A). ∎

3

Question 1.5.
We want to find $P(A) = 1 - P(A^c)$, where A is defined to be the event that "one integer is *not* the square of the other" and A^c is the complement of this event, i.e. A^c is the event that "one integer *is* the square of the other". Suppose the first coordinate of each ordered pair corresponds to Sofia's number and the second corresponds to Tess's. Then $A^c = \{(1,1), (2,4), (4,2), (3,9), (9,3)\}$ has five elements, and the sample space

$$\{(1,1), (1,2), \ldots, (1,10), \ldots, (10,10)\}$$

has a hundred elements. Thus, the probability that neither number selected is the square of the other must be

$$P(A) = 1 - P(A^c) = 1 - 0.05 = 0.95.$$

We fill in bubble (E) and continue. ∎

Question 1.6.
The function $f(x) := x^6$ increases monotonically on the interval $[0, \infty)$. This can be proven, for example, by taking the derivative. Because

$$f(2^{1/2}) = 8, \quad f(3^{1/3}) = 9, \quad \text{and} \quad f(6^{1/6}) = 6,$$

we conclude

$$6^{1/6} < 2^{1/2} < 3^{1/3}.$$

So, the answer is (C). ∎

Question 1.7.
Because f increases on the closed interval $[0, 2]$, and decreases on the closed interval $[2, 4]$, the value $f(2)$ must be an absolute maximum.

Using the *Fundamental theorem of Calculus*, we know

$$\int_0^4 f'(x)\, dx = f(4) - f(0).$$

4

Since the definite integral of f' from 0 to 4 measures the net signed area between f' and the x-axis over the interval, we conclude that the left side of the equation is positive, because the positive area between f' and the x-axis over the interval $(0, 2)$ has greater magnitude than the negative area between f' and the x-axis over the interval $(2, 4)$. It follows that $f(0) < f(4)$. Therefore,

$$f(0) < f(4) < f(2)$$

and we select (C). ■

Question 1.8. ───────────────────────

The nonzero integers under multiplication are not a *group* because the multiplicative inverses of some integers are not integers, e.g. $1/3$ is the multiplicative inverse of 3. Fill in the bubble for (B). ■

Question 1.9. ───────────────────────

Recall the geometric interpretation of the first and second derivatives. The value $g'(x)$ tells us the slope of g at x, and $g''(x)$ tells us the concavity of g at x. As a result, g is flat at $x = 0$, concave up at $x = -1$, and concave down on the open interval $(0, 2)$. Let's go through our options. Choice (B) fails because the graph is concave up on a subset of $(0, 2)$, (C) doesn't work because the graph isn't flat at $x = 0$, (D) can't be it because the graph is concave up on a subset of $(0, 2)$, and we remove (E) from consideration because the graph is concave down at $x = -1$. The only available option is (A). ■

Question 1.10. ───────────────────────

We will solve this problem using algebra:

$$\begin{aligned} \sqrt{(x+3)^2 + (y-2)^2} &= \sqrt{(x-3)^2 + y^2} \\ \Rightarrow \quad (x+3)^2 + (y-2)^2 &= (x-3)^2 + y^2 \\ \Rightarrow \quad x^2 + 6x + 9 + y^2 - 4y + 4 &= x^2 - 6x + 9 + y^2 \\ \Rightarrow \quad 12x - 4y &= -4. \end{aligned}$$

The answer is (A), because this is the equation of a line. ■

5

Question 1.11. ───────────────────────────────────

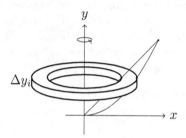

We will find a formula in terms of y_i for the volume of a thin washer ΔV_i, and then formulate the total volume as the limit of a Riemann sum of ΔV_i's.

Each slice of volume is the area of its annular cross-section multiplied by a small vertical length Δy_i. The outer radius of the annular cross-section lies on the curve $y = x^2$ and inner radius on the line $y = x$. Hence, at the y-value y_i the outer and inner radii are $\sqrt{y_i}$ and y_i, respectively. Thus,

$$\Delta V_i = \pi\left((\sqrt{y_i})^2 - (y_i)^2\right)\Delta y_i = \pi\left(y_i - (y_i)^2\right)\Delta y_i.$$

The minimum and maximum y-values, within the region bounded by $y = x$ and $y = x^2$, are 0 and 1, respectively. Consider the partition $P = \{1, 1/2, 1/3, \ldots, 1/(n+1)\}$ of the interval $[0, 1]$. Suppose $y_i = 1/(n-i+1)$ and $\Delta y_i = 1/(n-i+1) - 1/(n-i+2)$. Notice that $\sum_{i=1}^{n} \Delta V_i \approx V$. Furthermore, as $n \to \infty$, we have $\sum_{i=1}^{n} \Delta V_i \to V$ and

$$\sum_{i=1}^{n} \Delta V_i = \sum_{i=1}^{n} \pi\left(y_i - (y_i)^2\right)\Delta y_i \longrightarrow \int_0^1 \pi\left(y - y^2\right)dy.$$

Hence, the volume obtained from rotating the region bounded by $y = x$ and $y = x^2$ about the y-axis is

$$V = \int_0^1 \pi\left(y - y^2\right)\,dy = \pi\left[\frac{y^2}{2} - \frac{y^3}{3}\right]_0^1 = \frac{\pi}{6}.$$

We select (B) and continue. Note that we went through the reasoning behind the *washer method*. ■

Question 1.12. ────────────────────────────
Any group of prime order must be cyclic. This follows from *Lagrange's theorem* which says the order of a subgroup must divide the order of the entire group. So, if a group has prime order, then any nonidentity element must generate the entire group because it generates a subgroup of order other then 1.

It follows that all groups of prime order are isomorphic to all other groups of the same prime order. This is due to the fact that all prime ordered groups are cyclic and all cyclic groups of the same order are isomorphic.

It is easy enough to find groups that are non-isomorphic but of the same order for the composite values of n. For example, there are two groups, up to isomorphism, of order 9; they are $\mathbb{Z}_9$ and $\mathbb{Z}_3 \times \mathbb{Z}_3$.

Ergo, (B) must be the correct answer. ■

Question 1.13. ────────────────────────────
Due to an *integration property*, if $f'(x) \geq -1$ for all x, then

$$\int_0^3 f'(x) \, dx \geq \int_0^3 -1 \, dx = -3.$$

Because of the *Fundamental theorem of Calculus*,

$$\int_0^3 f'(x) \, dx = f(3) - f(0) = 5 - f(0).$$

Hence, $5 - f(0) \geq -3$. Solving for $f(0)$ yields $f(0) \leq 8$. We conclude that option (D) is correct. ■

Question 1.14. ────────────────────────────
Since there is no area under a point,

$$\int_c^c g(t) \, dt = 0.$$

Due to the given equation, it follows that $3c^5 + 96 = 0$. After a little algebra, we find that $c = -2$. Pick option (B). ■

Question 1.15. ─────────────────────────────────

The function f must be one-to-one. Suppose otherwise. Then there are unique elements s_1 and s_2 in S such that $f(s_1) = f(s_2)$. But this implies $(g \circ f)(s_1) = (g \circ f)(s_2)$, which is a contradiction of the assumption that $g \circ f$ is one-to-one.

During an the exam, this would be a good time to select (A) and continue, but let's find counterexamples for the others. Consider

$$f = \{(1,2)\} \quad \text{and} \quad g = \{(2,4),(3,4)\},$$

where

$$S = \{1\}, \quad T = \{2,3\}, \quad \text{and} \quad U = \{4,5\}.$$

The composite function $g \circ f = \{(1,4)\}$ is clearly one-to-one. However, the function f is not onto, because 3 is not in the image of f; g is not one-to-one because $g(2) = g(3)$; the function g is not onto because 5 is not in its range; and the image of $g \circ f$ does not contain 5 which means $g \circ f$ cannot be onto. ■

Question 1.16. ─────────────────────────────────

The first step is to clearly formulate this scenario as a conditional statement:

If either A or B, then C.

Note: most mathematicians consider *or* to be inclusive, so X *or* Y being true implies X could be true, Y could be true, or both X and Y could be true. The *either* in front makes the *or* exclusive.

Since the negation of *either A or B* is *A and B, or not A and not B*, the contrapositive of our conditional statement is

If not C, then $\big(A$ and $B\big)$ or $\big($not A and not $B\big)$.

In other words, when C is false, the statements A and B must have the same truth value. Thus, given that C is false, A being false implies that B is false. We choose (B). ■

Question 1.17. ————————————————————————

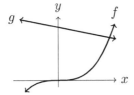

Let's reformulate the first option as a graphing problem. Suppose

$$f(x) := x^3 \quad \text{and} \quad g(x) := 10 - x.$$

The number of solutions to the equation in (A) is the same as the number of intersections of the graphs of f and g. So, after we draw a rough sketch of f and g, we see that the equation in (A) has one real solution.

Consider (B). We know

$$x^2 + 5x - 7 = x + 8 \quad \text{if and only if} \quad x^2 + 4x - 15 = 0.$$

The *discriminant* of the latter quadratic equation is $4^2 - 4(1)(-15) = 76 > 0$. This implies that there are two real solutions.

Algebra shows that the one solution of equation (C) is $x = -2/5$.

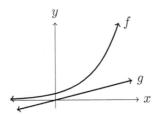

The number of real solutions of equation (D) is the same as the number of intersections of the graphs of

$$f(x) := e^x \quad \text{and} \quad g(x) := x.$$

A sketch shows that there are no intersections, so equation (D) has no real solution.

Since this is tougher to graph, a few remarks are in order. Notice that $f(x) > 0$ and $g(x) < 0$ for $x < 0$, which means there is no hope of the graphs intersecting for negative values of x. To prove there is no intersection for $x \geq 0$, notice

$$f(0) = e^0 = 1 \quad \text{and} \quad g(0) = 0,$$

while $f'(x) = e^x > 1$ and $g'(x) = 1$ for $x > 0$. In other words, f is bigger at $x = 0$ and grows faster for $x > 0$, so there is no chance of f and g intersecting for positive values of x.

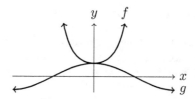

Examine (E). Notice

$$\sec x = e^{-x^2} \quad \text{if and only if} \quad e^{x^2} = \cos x.$$

So, the number of solutions of equation (E) is the same as the number of intersections of the graphs of

$$f(x) := e^{x^2} \quad \text{and} \quad g(x) := \cos x.$$

Because $f'(x) = 2xe^{x^2}$,

$$f'(x) < 0 \text{ for } x < 0 \quad \text{and} \quad f'(x) > 0 \text{ for } x > 0.$$

It follows that $f(0) = 1$ is the absolute minimum. Since $g(0) = \cos 0 = 1$, we conclude that the graphs intersect at $x = 0$. Since the range of g is the interval $[-1, 1]$, there are no other intersections. Note: a list of *sine and cosine values in quadrant I* is given in the glossary.

Therefore, equation (B) has the greatest number of solutions. Fill in the bubble and move on! ∎

Question 1.18. ─────────────────────────────
The function

$$f'(x) = \frac{d}{dx}\left(\sum_{n=1}^{\infty} \frac{x^n}{n}\right) = \sum_{n=1}^{\infty} \frac{1}{n} \cdot \frac{d}{dx}(x^n) = \sum_{n=1}^{\infty} x^{n-1}.$$

We need one of the *summation formulas* from Calculus:

$$\sum_{k=1}^{\infty} ar^{k-1} = \frac{a}{1-r}, \quad \text{when} \quad |r| < 1.$$

In our case, $a = 1$ and $r = x$, so

$$f'(x) = \frac{1}{1-x}.$$

We select (A) and proceed to the next question. ∎

Question 1.19. ─────────────────────────────
For any complex number z,

$$z = |z|e^{i\theta} = |z|\left(\cos\theta + i\sin\theta\right),$$

where $|z|$ is the modulus of z and θ is some number in the interval $(-\pi, \pi]$. Using the identity, we see

$$\bar{z} = |z|\left(\cos\theta - i\sin\theta\right) = |z|\left(\cos(-\theta) + i\sin(-\theta)\right) = |z|e^{-i\theta},$$

because $\cos\theta = \cos(-\theta)$ and $-\sin\theta = \sin(-\theta)$. Furthermore, notice that $z \to 0$ is equivalent to saying $|z| \to 0$. We are ready to compute our limit:

$$\lim_{z \to 0} \frac{(\bar{z})^2}{z^2} = \lim_{|z| \to 0} \frac{\left(|z|e^{-i\theta}\right)^2}{\left(|z|e^{i\theta}\right)^2}$$

$$= \lim_{|z| \to 0} \frac{e^{-2i\theta}}{e^{2i\theta}}$$

$$= e^{-4i\theta}.$$

Since θ could be any value in the interval $(-\pi, \pi]$, the limit does not exist and we pick option (E). ∎

11

Question 1.20. ————————————————————————————
The limit is in the $0/0$ indeterminate form, because the numerator
is $g(g(0)) - g(e) = g(e) - g(e) = 0$ and the denominator is 0 when
$x = 0$. So, we will use *L'Hôpital's rule*. We continue as follows:

$$\lim_{x \to 0} \frac{g(g(x)) - g(e)}{x} \overset{LH}{=} \lim_{x \to 0} \frac{g'(g(x))g'(x) - 0}{1} = g'(g(0))g'(0).$$

Since $g'(x) = 2e^{2x+1}$, we have

$$g'(g(0))g'(0) = g'(e) \cdot 2e = 2e^{2e+1} \cdot 2e = 4e^{2e+2}.$$

Thus, the correct answer must be (E). ∎

Question 1.21. ————————————————————————————
We first prove that $\sqrt{1 + t^2} \sin^3 t \cos^3 t$ is odd:

$$\sqrt{1 + (-t)^2} \sin^3(-t) \cos^3(-t) = \sqrt{1 + t^2}(-\sin t)^3 \cos^3 t$$
$$= -\sqrt{1 + t^2} \sin^3 t \cos^3 t.$$

If f is an odd function, then $\int_{-a}^{a} f(t) \, dt = 0$ for all real numbers a
for which the integral makes sense. This is because the signed area
to the left of the origin has the same magnitude, but the opposite
sign, as the area to the right of the origin.

With this and our basic *integration properties* in mind, we compute
the definite integral:

$$\int_{-\pi/4}^{\pi/4} \left(\cos t + \sqrt{1 + t^2} \sin^3 t \cos^3 t \right) dt$$

$$= \int_{-\pi/4}^{\pi/4} \cos t \, dt + \int_{-\pi/4}^{\pi/4} \sqrt{1 + t^2} \sin^3 t \cos^3 t \, dt$$

$$= \int_{-\pi/4}^{\pi/4} \cos t \, dt + 0$$

$$= \sin t \Big|_{-\pi/4}^{\pi/4}$$

$$= \sin(\pi/4) - \sin(-\pi/4)$$

$$= \sqrt{2}.$$

Choose (B) and move on. Note: there is a list of *sine and cosine values in quadrant I* located in the glossary. ■

Question 1.22. ───────────────────────────
The first step is to draw the base of the solid.

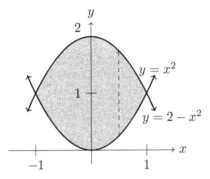

We observe that the planes $z = y + 3$ and $z = 0$ never intersect within the region above. It follows that the volume is

$$V = \int_{-1}^{1} \int_{x^2}^{2-x^2} \int_{0}^{y+3} dz\,dy\,dx$$

$$= \int_{-1}^{1} \int_{x^2}^{2-x^2} y + 3 \ dy\,dx$$

$$= \int_{-1}^{1} \frac{(2-x^2)^2}{2} + 3(2-x^2) - \frac{x^4}{2} - 3x^2 \ dx$$

$$= \int_{-1}^{1} \frac{x^4}{2} - 5x^2 + 8 - \frac{x^4}{2} - 3x^2 \ dx$$

$$= \int_{-1}^{1} 8 - 8x^2 \ dx$$

$$= \frac{32}{3}.$$

The correct answer is (C). ■

13

Question 1.23.

Consider the following addition and multiplication tables for S:

+	0	2	4	6	8
0	0	2	4	6	8
2	2	4	6	8	0
4	4	6	8	0	2
6	6	8	0	2	4
8	8	0	2	4	6

and

·	0	2	4	6	8
0	0	0	0	0	0
2	0	4	8	2	6
4	0	8	6	4	2
6	0	2	4	6	8
8	0	6	2	8	4.

It is easy to see that S is closed under $+$ and $\cdot$, 0 is the identity element under $+$, 6 is the identity element under $\cdot$, and both operations are commutative. Ergo, statement (D) is false. ∎

Question 1.24.

Let's reformulate the problem using matrices. Define

$$A := \begin{pmatrix} 1 & 3 & 2 & 2 \\ 1 & 4 & 1 & 0 \\ 3 & 5 & 10 & 14 \\ 2 & 5 & 5 & 6 \end{pmatrix} \quad \text{and} \quad x := \begin{pmatrix} w \\ x \\ y \\ z \end{pmatrix}.$$

Then our system can be written as $Ax = 0$.

Statement (A) is true. For any homogeneous system, where the dimension makes sense, $x = 0$ is a solution.

Statement (C) is true. Suppose $x = b$ and $x = c$ are solutions to $Ax = 0$. Then

$$A(b + c) = Ab + Ac = 0 + 0 = 0.$$

A quick computation shows that (D) is true:

$$
\begin{array}{rcccccccl}
-5 & + & 3(1) & + & 2(1) & + & 2(0) & = & 0 \\
-5 & + & 4(1) & + & 1 & & & = & 0 \\
3(-5) & + & 5(1) & + & 10(1) & + & 14(0) & = & 0 \\
2(-5) & + & 5(1) & + & 5(1) & + & 6(0) & = & 0.
\end{array}
$$

Statement (B) follows from (D). If there is a vector $b \neq 0$ such that $Ab = 0$, then for each scalar k in $\mathbb{R}$ the vector kb is a solution because

$$A(k\boldsymbol{b}) = kA\boldsymbol{b} = k \cdot \boldsymbol{0} = \boldsymbol{0}.$$

By the process of elimination, (E) must be false so we select it. We don't recommend that you find another solution to the system during the exam because it's somewhat time-consuming and it's very easy to make a mistake. That said, $\boldsymbol{x} = (-8, 2, 0, 1)$ is also a solution and it is not a scalar multiple of $(-5, 1, 1, 0)$. ■

Question 1.25. —————————————————————————————
This question is primarily testing your memory. Recall that $(c, h(c))$ is an *inflection point* of h if and only if h'' switches signs at c.

The value of h'' is positive when h' is increasing, and h'' is negative when h' is decreasing. Since h' goes from decreasing to increasing within the open interval $(-2, -1)$, there is a c in the interval such that $(c, h(c))$ is an inflection point. Fill in the bubble for (A)! ■

Question 1.26. —————————————————————————————
Since

$$4 \cdot 3 \equiv 12 \equiv 1 \pmod{11} \quad \text{and} \quad 6 \cdot 2 \equiv 12 \equiv 1 \pmod{11},$$

the multiplicative inverses of 3 and 2 are 4 and 6, respectively. So,

$$
\begin{aligned}
3x &\equiv 5 \pmod{11} \quad &\text{and} \quad 2y &\equiv 7 \pmod{11} \\
\Rightarrow 12x &\equiv 20 \pmod{11} \quad &\text{and} \quad 12y &\equiv 42 \pmod{11} \\
\Rightarrow \quad x &\equiv 9 \pmod{11} \quad &\text{and} \quad y &\equiv 9 \pmod{11}.
\end{aligned}
$$

Thus,

$$
\begin{aligned}
x + y &\equiv 9 + 9 \\
&\equiv 18 \\
&\equiv 7 \pmod{11}.
\end{aligned}
$$

The correct answer must be (D). ■

Question 1.27. ―――――――――――――――――――――

Recall the following identity. Suppose $z \neq 0$ is a complex number. Then

$$z = |z|e^{i\theta} = |z|\left(\cos\theta + i\sin\theta\right),$$

where $|z|$ is the modulus of z and θ is some number in the interval $(-\pi, \pi]$.

Our goal is to write $z = 1 + i$ into the form $|z|e^{i\theta}$, use exponent rules to raise z to the 10th power, and then use the expression with trigonometric functions to write our result in standard form.

Let's find the modulus of z:

$$|z| = \sqrt{1^2 + 1^2} = \sqrt{2}.$$

Therefore,

$$z = \sqrt{2}\left(\frac{1}{\sqrt{2}} + \frac{i}{\sqrt{2}}\right) = \sqrt{2}\left(\frac{\sqrt{2}}{2} + i\frac{\sqrt{2}}{2}\right).$$

It follows that $\cos\theta = \sqrt{2}/2$ and $\sin\theta = \sqrt{2}/2$. From what we know about the unit circle, or by inspection of the list of *sine and cosine values in quadrant I* in the glossary, we can conclude that $\theta = \pi/4$. The rest of the problem is a simple computation:

$$(1 + i)^{10} = \left(\sqrt{2}e^{\pi i/4}\right)^{10}$$
$$= 2^5 e^{5\pi i/2}$$
$$= 32\left(\cos\frac{5\pi}{2} + i\sin\frac{5\pi}{2}\right)$$
$$= 32\left(0 + 1i\right)$$
$$= 32i.$$

The solution must be (D). ∎

Question 1.28. ———————————————————————————

We know
$$y - 4 = 3(x - 1) \quad \text{implies} \quad y = 3x + 1.$$

Because f is tangent to $y = 3x + 1$ at $x = 1$, $f(1) = 3(1) + 1 = 4$ and $f'(1) = 3$. This allows us to jettison (A) as an option.

The *inverse function theorem* says

> Suppose f has a continuous non-zero derivative in some connected open neighborhood of $x = a$. Further, assume the graph of f within this neighborhood contains the point (a, b). Then
> $$(f^{-1})'(b) = \frac{1}{f'(a)}.$$

We note that injectivity of the differentiable function f implies f' is non-zero in a connected neighborhood of $x = 1$. It follows that $(f^{-1})'(4) = 1/3$. We remove (B) from consideration.

With the *derivative rules* from Calculus in mind, the last three options are simple computations.

Using the product rule,
$$(fg)'(1) = f(1)g'(1) + f'(1)g(1)$$
$$= 4 \left(\frac{1}{2\sqrt{1}} \right) + 3 \left(\sqrt{1} \right)$$
$$= 2 + 3$$
$$= 5.$$

So we eliminate (C).

Option (D) is false, so we select it. The untruth of (D) is proven using the chain rule:
$$(g \circ f)'(1) = g'(f(1)) \cdot f'(1)$$
$$= g'(4) \cdot 3$$
$$= \left(\frac{1}{2\sqrt{4}} \right) \cdot 3$$
$$= 3/4$$
$$\neq 1/2.$$

The last one, (E), is true. We have

$$(g \circ f)(1) = g\,(f(1))$$
$$= g(4)$$
$$= \sqrt{4}$$
$$= 2.$$

∎

Question 1.29. ——————————————————————————
Let's go through the cases. It is clear that we can connect at most four edges to a vertex of our tree.

The next possibility is that one of the vertices has three edges connected to it.

The last case we need to consider is when there are no more than two edges connect to each vertex.

Ergo, there are three non-isomorphic trees with five vertices, so (C) is the correct answer. ∎

Question 1.30. ────────────────────────────

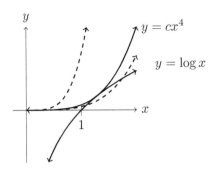

As can be seen above, if the graph of $y = cx^4$ and $y = \log x$ intersect at exactly one point, then the graphs are tangent at their intersection. Being tangent at a location implies that they have the same slope, which means the derivatives of the two functions are equal. So,

$$\frac{1}{x} = 4cx^3 \quad \text{implies} \quad x = \sqrt[4]{\frac{1}{4c}}.$$

Hence,

$$\log x = cx^4$$
$$\Rightarrow \quad \log\left(\sqrt[4]{\frac{1}{4c}}\right) = c \cdot \frac{1}{4c}$$
$$\Rightarrow \quad \frac{1}{4}\log\left(\frac{1}{4c}\right) = \frac{1}{4}$$
$$\Rightarrow \quad \log\left(\frac{1}{4c}\right) = 1$$
$$\Rightarrow \quad \frac{1}{4c} = e$$
$$\Rightarrow \quad c = \frac{1}{4e}.$$

And we have proven that the answer is (A). A list of *logarithm properties* is located in the glossary. ∎

Question 1.31.
To find the eigenvalues, we need to find the characteristic polynomial

$$p(\lambda) = \det \begin{pmatrix} 3-\lambda & 5 & 3 \\ 1 & 7-\lambda & 3 \\ 1 & 2 & 8-\lambda \end{pmatrix} = -(\lambda-2)(\lambda-5)(\lambda-11).$$

The eigenvalues are the solutions of $p(\lambda) = 0$. Thus, we select (C), because 2 and 5 are eigenvalues but not 3. ∎

Question 1.32.
Recall the *Fundamental theorem of Calculus*:

Suppose f is continuous on the closed interval $[a,b]$. Then

$$\int_a^b f(t)\, dt = F(b) - F(a),$$

where $F'(t) = f(t)$.

Supposed $F(t)$ is an antiderivative of e^{t^2}. Then

$$\frac{d}{dx} \int_{x^3}^{x^4} e^{t^2}\, dt = \frac{d}{dx}\left(F(x^4) - F(x^3) \right)$$
$$= 4x^3 F'(x^4) - 3x^2 F'(x^3)$$
$$= 4x^3 e^{x^8} - 3x^2 e^{x^6}$$
$$= x^2 e^{x^6} \left(4x e^{x^8 - x^6} - 3 \right).$$

Select (E). A list of *derivative rules* is located in the glossary. ∎

Question 1.33.
We will rewrite the ratio as a product and use the product rule, which is one of the *derivative rules* in the glossary. Let

$$f(x) := \frac{x-1}{e^x} = (x-1)e^{-x}.$$

So,

$$f'(x) = 1e^{-x} - (x-1)e^{-x} \qquad f''(x) = -1e^{-x} + (x-2)e^{-x}$$
$$= (2-x)e^{-x} \qquad\qquad\qquad = (x-3)e^{-x},$$
$$= -(x-2)e^{-x},$$

and

$$f'''(x) = e^{-x} - (x-3)e^{-x}$$
$$= (4-x)e^{-x}$$
$$= -(x-4)e^{-x}.$$

It appears that

$$f^{(n)}(x) = (-1)^n(x-n-1)e^{-x}.$$

To prove this, we would use induction on n. However, proofs aren't necessary for the GRE and this result seems sufficiently self-evident. We conclude

$$f^{(19)}(x) = -(x-20)e^{-x} = (20-x)e^{-x},$$

and we fill in the bubble for (C). ∎

Question 1.34. ————————————————————————————
Let's compute $\det(A)$. There is a theorem that says the determinant of an upper or lower triangular matrix is the product of the entries on the main diagonal. Therefore,

$$\det(A) = 1 \cdot 2 \cdot 3 \cdot 4 \cdot 5 = 120.$$

We can immediately exclude (E) as a possibility. Furthermore, since a matrix is invertible if and only if the determinant is non-zero, A is invertible and we jettison (A). We remove (D) as a possibility because there is a sequence of elementary row operations that can be used to transform A into the identity; one algorithm to find the inverse is to consider $(A|I)$ and perform elementary row operations until you find $(I|A^{-1})$ so (D) is also equivalent to asking whether A is invertible.

Let's turn our attention to (B). It is not too hard to see that the proposition $A\boldsymbol{x} = \boldsymbol{x}$ implies $\boldsymbol{x} = \boldsymbol{0}$ is equivalent to the claim that 1 is *not* an eigenvalue of A. We will show that 1 is an eigenvalue by proving that it is a zero of the characteristic polynomial. Since

$$p(\lambda) = \det \begin{pmatrix} 1-\lambda & 2 & 3 & 4 & 5 \\ 0 & 2-\lambda & 3 & 4 & 5 \\ 0 & 0 & 3-\lambda & 4 & 5 \\ 0 & 0 & 0 & 4-\lambda & 5 \\ 0 & 0 & 0 & 0 & 5-\lambda \end{pmatrix},$$

we know

$$p(1) = \det \begin{pmatrix} 0 & 2 & 3 & 4 & 5 \\ 0 & 1 & 3 & 4 & 5 \\ 0 & 0 & 2 & 4 & 5 \\ 0 & 0 & 0 & 3 & 5 \\ 0 & 0 & 0 & 0 & 4 \end{pmatrix} = 0.$$

Select (B) as your answer.

Since we are not being timed (now) we will show that (C) is valid. The last row of A^2 is

$$(0\,0\,0\,0\,5) \begin{pmatrix} 1 & 2 & 3 & 4 & 5 \\ 0 & 2 & 3 & 4 & 5 \\ 0 & 0 & 3 & 4 & 5 \\ 0 & 0 & 0 & 4 & 5 \\ 0 & 0 & 0 & 0 & 5 \end{pmatrix} = (0\,0\,0\,0\,25).$$

$\blacksquare$

Question 1.35. ────────────────────────────
We would like to find the point on the plane $2x + y + 3z = 3$ that is closest to the origin. This is equivalent to finding the point (x, y, x) on the plane that minimizes $d(x, y, z) = \sqrt{x^2 + y^2 + z^2}$. Since square roots increase monotonically, the point that minimizes d will also minimize $f(x, y, x) := x^2 + y^2 + z^2$. As such, for simplicity, we will minimize $f(x, y, z) = x^2 + y^2 + z^2$ subject to the constraint $g(x, y, z) := 2x + y + 3z = 3$. Via the *method of Lagrange multipliers*, we know relative extrema occur when

$$\nabla f(x, y, z) = \lambda \nabla g(x, y, z),$$

22

for some λ. It follows that

$$2x = 2\lambda, \quad 2y = \lambda, \quad \text{and} \quad 2z = 3\lambda.$$

A bit of algebra shows that $y = x/2$, and $z = 3x/2$. Thus,

$$3 = g\left(x, \frac{x}{2}, \frac{3x}{2}\right)$$

$$= 2x + \left(\frac{x}{2}\right) + 3\left(\frac{3x}{2}\right)$$

$$= 7x.$$

Hence, $x = 3/7$, $y = 3/14$, and $z = 9/14$. The minimum is a relative extremum, because there is a disk on the plane containing the closest point such that every other point in the disk is farther away from the origin. Since $(3/7, 3/14, 9/14)$ is the only relative extremum, it must minimize f. Thus, (B) is correct. ■

Question 1.36. ────────────────────────────

Option (A) need not be true. Consider $S = \{0, 1\}$. There is no continuous function from the closed interval $[0, 1]$ to S.

Option (B) is not the solution. Consider $S = (0, 1)$. Since 0 is a limit point of S, there is no open neighborhood U of 0 such that $U \cap S = \varnothing$.

Option (C) must be true, which means this is the correct answer. Let

$$W := \{v \in S : \exists \text{ an open } V \subseteq \mathbb{R} \text{ s.t. } v \in V \subseteq S\}.$$

If W is empty, then we are done because the empty set is open. Suppose not and consider v in W. By definition, there is an open neighborhood V of v such that $V \subseteq S$. For u in V, we have u in W, because there exists an open subset of u contained within S, namely V. It follows that each point of W has an open neighborhood contained within W. Thus, W is open.

Option (D) is not always true. Consider $S = [0, 1]$. It is not too tough to see that

$$\{w \notin S : \exists \text{ an open } W \subseteq \mathbb{R} \text{ s.t. } w \in W, W \cap S = \varnothing\} = (-\infty, 0) \cup (1, \infty)$$

is open.

Option (E) is out. When S is open, it cannot be recreated via the intersections of closed subsets, because the intersection of closed subsets is always closed. ∎

Question 1.37. ────────────────────────────

Statement I is false. Consider the case where $P : \mathbb{R} \to \mathbb{R}$ such that $P : x \mapsto 0$. Then $P^2 : x \mapsto 0$. It follows that $P^2 = P$, but P is not invertible.

Statement II is true. Consider v in V. Then $v = (v - Pv) + Pv$. Since

$$P(v - Pv) = Pv - P^2 v = Pv - Pv = \mathbf{0},$$

so we can write every element of V as the sum of a vector in the null space of P and a vector in the range of P. Furthermore, the vectors in the range of P are invariant under P because $P(Pv) = P^2 v = Pv$, which implies vectors in the range are eigenvectors with an eigenvalue of 1. Clearly, vectors in the null space of P are eigenvectors with an eigenvalue of 0. We can conclude that P is diagonalizable because there exists a basis of eigenvectors, namely a basis for the null space of P union a basis for the range of P.

Statement III is false. There do exist linear transformations such that $P^2 = P$, but P is not the identity or the zero transformation. For example, if

$$P = \begin{pmatrix} 1 & 0 \\ 0 & 0 \end{pmatrix} \quad \text{then} \quad P^2 = \begin{pmatrix} 1 & 0 \\ 0 & 0 \end{pmatrix}.$$

We select (C). ∎

Question 1.38. ────────────────────────────

We know that the sum of the interior angles of an n-gon is $180°(n-1)$. This implies that the sum of the interior angles of our 10-gon is $180°(8) = 1440°$. Since our polygon is convex, all interior angles must have measure less than $180°$. We will consider the degenerate case, where there are m angles of measure $90°$ and n angles of

24

measure $180°$. We know $m + n = 10$ because there are ten i.
angles. So, we will solve

$$\begin{cases} 90°m + 180°n & = 1440° \\ m + n & = 10. \end{cases}$$

This yields $m = 4$ and $n = 6$. Since our obtuse angles must have
measure less than $180°$ and our acute angles must have measure
less than $90°$, this is an impossibility. However, if we make one
of our $90°$ angles obtuse, then we can decrease the measures of
the $180°$ angles and the other $90°$ angles by a small amount. This
yields the optimal number of acute angles in our 10-gon. Thus,
there can be at most three acute angles. And we have proven (C)
is correct. ∎

Question 1.39. ————————————————————————
The solution is (D). We input n=88. The algorithm sets i=1. Since
i=1 is less than n=88, we enter the first while loop. This changes
i to 2, and sets k=n=88. Because k=88 is greater than or equal
to i=2, we enter the second while loop which reduces k by 1 each
iteration, until k=i=2. At this time i=2 is printed, and we go back
to the beginning of the first while loop. This process continues up
to i=88, at which time the criterion for the second while loop will
pass for the last time which will result in 88 being printed. Then
we go back to the first while loop which increases i to 89. Because
i=89 is not less than k=88, we will not enter the second while loop.
As a result, no more numbers will be printed. ∎

Question 1.40. ————————————————————————
Statement III is true, and the others are false. To disprove I and
II, consider

$$f(x) := 1, \quad g(x) := 2, \quad \text{and} \quad h(x) := 1 + x.$$

We can disprove commutativity of ∘ by considering

$$(f \circ g)(x) = 1 \quad \text{and} \quad (g \circ f)(x) = 2.$$

Furthermore, we disprove that ∘ is distributive on the left via considering

$$f \circ (g+h) = f(3+x) = 1 \quad \text{and} \quad (f \circ g)(x) + (f \circ h)(x) = 1+1 = 2.$$

The truth of statement III follows directly from the definition of function addition. By definition,

$$(g+h)(x) := g(x) + h(x).$$

Replace the quantity x with $f(x)$ within this definition and the result follows. Fill in (C) and continue. ∎

Question 1.41.

To find an equation of this plane, we need a point on the plane (which we have), and a vector normal to the plane.

To find a normal vector, we construct a vector parallel to ℓ. Solving the system

$$\begin{cases} x + y + z &= 3 \\ x - y + z &= 5 \end{cases},$$

shows that any point of the form $(4 - t, -1, t)$, for t a real number, lies on ℓ. Any vector with tip and tail on ℓ will be parallel, so we select two values of t and find the vector between them. Letting $t = 0$ yields the point $(4, -1, 0)$. Letting $t = 1$ yields the point $(3, -1, 1)$. It follows that the vector

$$\boldsymbol{u} := \left(4 - 3, -1 - (-1), 0 - 1\right) = \left(1, 0, -1\right)$$

is parallel to ℓ, and therefore perpendicular to the plane.

We are ready to construct the plane. Suppose (x, y, x) is a point on it. Then the vector

$$\boldsymbol{v} := \left(x - 0, y - 0, z - 0\right) = \left(x, y, z\right)$$

lies on the plane. Let's compute the dot product of $\boldsymbol{u}$ and $\boldsymbol{v}$:

$$\boldsymbol{u} \cdot \boldsymbol{v} = \left(1, 0, -1\right) \cdot \left(x, y, z\right) = x - z.$$

26

Since u and v are orthogonal, $u \cdot v = 0$. Hence, an equation for the plane is $x - z = 0$. The correct answer must be (A). ∎

Question 1.42.

All of the propositions listed are true. This metric induces the discrete topology on $\mathbb{Z}^+$, and within this topology, every set is both open and closed. This forces all functions with domain $\mathbb{Z}^+$ to be continuous, because the inverse image of an open set will, no doubt, be open (since all sets in the domain are open). However, let's go through our options supposing that we don't know about the discrete topology.

Proposition I: For each n in $\mathbb{Z}^+$, the open ball centered at n of radius $1/2$ is contained within $\{n\}$. It follows that every point of $\{n\}$ is an interior point, which proves that $\{n\}$ is open.

Proposition II: Consider an arbitrary set $A \subseteq \mathbb{Z}^+$. We will prove it's closed by showing that the complement $\mathbb{Z}^+ \setminus A$ is open. Because of proposition I, we know all singleton sets are open. Furthermore, the union of open sets is open and

$$\bigcup_{n \in \mathbb{Z}^+ \setminus A} \{n\} = \mathbb{Z}^+ \setminus A.$$

It follows that the complement of A is open, so A is closed.

Proposition III: Recall the ε-δ definition of continuity for real-valued functions: A function $f : X \to \mathbb{R}$ is continuous at c if and only if for all $\varepsilon > 0$ there exists a $\delta > 0$ such that

$$|f(x) - f(c)| < \varepsilon \quad \text{whenever} \quad d_X(x,c) < \delta,$$

where d_X is the metric on X. This criterion clearly holds for any real-valued function with domain $\mathbb{Z}^+$ given our metric; simply let $\delta = 1/2$, and it follows vacuously.

Hence, we select (E). ∎

Question 1.43. ─────────────────────────────────

We need to find the second derivative of y with respect to x. It would be a mess to remove the parameter. Instead, recall the following two Calculus formulas for the *slope and concavity of curves with parametric equations*:

> Suppose $x = f(t)$ and $y = g(t)$ describe a curve. Then the slope and concavity of the curve at the point corresponding to t, respectively, are
>
> $$\frac{dy}{dx} = \frac{dy/dt}{dx/dt} \quad \text{and} \quad \frac{d^2y}{dx^2} = \frac{d^2y/dtdx}{dx/dt}.$$

It is not hard to see that $dy/dt = 12t^3 + 12t^2$ and $dx/dt = 2t + 2$, so

$$\frac{dy}{dx} = \frac{12t^3 + 12t^2}{2t + 2} = 6t^2.$$

Then $d^2y/dtdx = 12t$. Hence,

$$\frac{d^2y}{dx^2} = \frac{12t}{2t + 2} = \frac{6t}{t + 1}.$$

Our next task is to find the t corresponding to the point $(8, 80)$. Since $x(t) = t^2 + 2t = 8$, $t = -4$ or $t = 2$. Of these two values of t, it is not a difficult computation to conclude that $t = 2$ is the only one that satisfies $y(t) = 3t^4 + 4t^3 = 80$. Hence,

$$\left.\frac{d^2y}{dx^2}\right|_{t=2} = \frac{6(2)}{2 + 1} = 4.$$

Fill in the bubble for (A).   ■

Question 1.44. ────────────────────────────────

Let's find the general solution to our differential equation. To do this, we will separate variables:

$$y' + xy = x \quad \text{implies} \quad \frac{y'}{y-1} = -x.$$

Then we integrate both sides with respect to x. On the left side, we have

$$\int \frac{y'}{y-1}\, dx = \int \frac{dy}{y-1} = \log|y-1|.$$

We omit the C, because only one is necessary per equation. On the right side, we have

$$\int -x\, dx = -\frac{x^2}{2} + C.$$

Hence,

$$\log|y-1| = -\frac{x^2}{2} + C$$

$$\Rightarrow \quad y - 1 = \pm e^{-x^2/2 + C}$$

$$\Rightarrow \quad y = \pm e^{C} e^{-x^2/2} + 1$$

$$= K e^{-x^2/2} + 1,$$

where $K = \pm e^{C}$. Since

$$\lim_{x \to -\infty} y(x) = \lim_{x \to -\infty} 1 + K e^{-x^2/2} = 1,$$

regardless of K, we need not bother finding it. We conclude that the answer is (B). ■

Question 1.45. ───────────────────────────────────

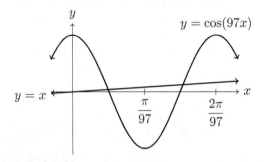

During the first quarter of each period cosine goes from 1 to 0, and in the fourth quarter cosine goes from 0 to 1. When $0 \leq x \leq 1$, this implies that the graphs of $y = \cos(97x)$ and $y = x$ intersect once in the first and fourth quarter of each period. The graph above illustrates this for the period within the interval $[0, 2\pi/97]$. When $x > 1$, $y = x$ will never intersect $y = \cos(97x)$.

As a result, we can find the number of intersections by computing the number of periods of $y = \cos(97x)$ within the interval $[0, 1]$. The period of $y = \cos(97x)$ is $2\pi/97$. It follows that there are

$$\frac{1}{2\pi/97} = \frac{97}{2\pi} \approx 15.4$$

periods between $x = 0$ and $x = 1$. Since $15.25 < 15.4 < 15.75$, $y = \cos(97x)$ and $y = x$ intersect $2(15) + 1 = 31$ times within our interval. Thus, the correct answer is (C). ■

Question 1.46. ───────────────────────────────────

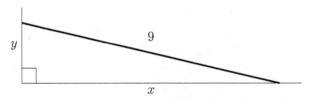

Let the variables be as shown. We omit units until our conclusion. We know $dx/dt = 2$ because x is increasing at a rate of 2. Our

30

goal is to find the magnitude of $dy/dt|_{y=3}$. Using the Pythagorean theorem, we know $x^2 + y^2 = 81$. Via implicit differentiation,

$$2x\frac{dx}{dt} + 2y\frac{dy}{dt} = 0,$$

and solving for dy/dt yields

$$\frac{dy}{dt} = -\frac{x}{y} \cdot \frac{dx}{dt}.$$

The Pythagorean theorem tells us $x = \sqrt{81 - 9} = 6\sqrt{2}$ when $y = 3$. Hence,

$$\frac{dy}{dt}\bigg|_{y=3} = -\frac{6\sqrt{2}}{3} \cdot 2 = -4\sqrt{2}.$$

We conclude that the ladder is sliding down the wall at a rate of $4\sqrt{2}$ meters per second. Pick (C). ∎

Question 1.47. ──────────────────────────────
We will first deal with continuity. We know $\lim_{x \to a} f(x) = L$ if and only if for each sequence $\{x_n\}_{n=1}^{\infty}$ such that $x_n \to a$ as $n \to \infty$, we have $\lim_{n \to \infty} f(x_n) = L$. Suppose a is a real number, and f is continuous at a. The claim that f is continuous at a is equivalent to saying $\lim_{x \to a} f(x) = f(a)$. Let $\{r_n\}_{n=1}^{\infty}$ be a sequence of rational numbers such that $r_n \to a$ as $n \to \infty$. Then

$$\lim_{x \to a} f(x) = \lim_{n \to \infty} f(r_n)$$
$$= \lim_{n \to \infty} 3r_n^2$$
$$= 3a^2.$$

Let $\{y_n\}_{n=1}^{\infty}$ be a sequence of irrational numbers such that $y_n \to a$ as $n \to \infty$. Then

$$\lim_{x \to a} f(x) = \lim_{n \to \infty} f(y_n)$$
$$= \lim_{n \to \infty} -5y_n^2$$
$$= -5a^2.$$

These two results must be equal, if f is continuous at a. It follows that $3a^2 = -5a^2$, which implies $a = 0$. We conclude that f is only continuous at 0.

Differentiability is a stronger claim than continuity. As a result, f is either differentiable nowhere or only at 0. We will use the derivative definition to determine differentiability at 0:

$$\begin{aligned} f'(0) &:= \lim_{h \to 0} \frac{f(h) - f(0)}{h} \\ &= \lim_{h \to 0} \frac{f(h) - 0}{h} \\ &= \lim_{h \to 0} \frac{f(h)}{h} \\ &= 0, \end{aligned}$$

because

$$\frac{f(h)}{h} = \begin{cases} 3h & \text{if } h \in \mathbb{Q} \setminus \{0\} \\ -5h & \text{if } h \notin \mathbb{Q} \end{cases} \to 0 \quad \text{as} \quad h \to 0.$$

We select (B). ■

Question 1.48. ─────────────────────────────

Recall the definition of the directional derivative:

> Suppose all first order partial derivatives of f exist at the point P. Then the directional derivative of f in the direction of $\boldsymbol{u} \neq \boldsymbol{0}$ is
>
> $$D_{\boldsymbol{u}} f|_P := \nabla f|_P \bullet \frac{\boldsymbol{u}}{|\boldsymbol{u}|},$$
>
> where $\bullet$ denotes the dot product.

It is not too tough to show that $\nabla g = (6xy, 3x^2, 1)$, which implies $\nabla g|_{(0,0,\pi)} = (0, 0, 1)$. Furthermore, if $\boldsymbol{u} = (1, 2, 3)$, then

$$\frac{\boldsymbol{u}}{|\boldsymbol{u}|} = \left(\frac{1}{\sqrt{14}}, \frac{2}{\sqrt{14}}, \frac{3}{\sqrt{14}} \right).$$

Hence,

$$D_{\boldsymbol{u}}g|_{(0,0,\pi)} = (0,0,1) \cdot \left(\frac{1}{\sqrt{14}}, \frac{2}{\sqrt{14}}, \frac{3}{\sqrt{14}} \right) = \frac{3}{\sqrt{14}}.$$

Tortuously, we still need to approximate the directional derivative. It is clear

$$\frac{3}{\sqrt{16}} < \frac{3}{\sqrt{14}} < \frac{3}{\sqrt{9}} \quad \text{implies} \quad 0.75 < \frac{3}{\sqrt{14}} < 1.$$

The only value within this range is 0.8, so we select (B). ■

Question 1.49. ───────────────────────────────

Every element of the symmetric group of n elements can be written as the product of disjoint cycles. Furthermore, the order of the product of disjoint cycles is the least common multiple of the orders of the cycles. This is because we must raise the product to the smallest number that has every cycle's order as a factor to obtain the minimal number which reduces the product to the identity element.

To illustrate this we will provide two examples. The product $(1, 2, 3)(4, 5)$ has order 6 because the first cycle in the product has order 3 and the second has order 2, so the product must be raised to the least common multiple of these numbers, i.e. 6, to reduce it to the identity element. In contrast, $(1, 2)(3, 4)(5)$ has order 2, because the orders of the cycles are 2, 2, and 1, and the least common multiple of these numbers is 2. Note that disjoint cycles will permute unique elements, so the sum of the orders of the cycles must be 5.

Our task, therefore, is to find integers m_i that maximize the least common multiple of the m_i, given that $\sum_i m_i = 5$. Let's go through the cases: lcm(5)=5, lcm(1,4)=4, lcm(2,3)=6, lcm(1,1,3)=3, lcm(1,2,2)=2, lcm(1,1,1,2)=2, and lcm(1,1,1,1,1)=1. Hence, the least common multiple is maximized at a value of 6. We conclude that the solution is (B). ■

Question 1.50. ——————————————————————————
Only I and III are ideals.

I: It is not too tough to see that $U + V$ remains a subring. It is also an ideal: Suppose r is in R, u is in U, and v is in V. By definition of an ideal, ru is in U and rv is in V. It follows that $r(u + v) = ru + rv$ is in $U + V$. This proves that $U + V$ is a left ideal. The argument to prove that $U + V$ is a right ideal is nearly identical.

II: For u_1 and u_2 in U and v_1 and v_2 in V, we cannot guarantee that $u_1 v_1 + u_2 v_2$ is in $U \cdot V$. Hence, it is not generally true that $U \cdot V$ is a subring. Since all ideals are subrings, $U \cdot V$ need not be an ideal. For example, consider the ring $\mathbb{R}[x, y]$ which is defined to be set of polynomials with variables x and y. Then $U = V = \{xp + yq : p, q \in \mathbb{R}[x, y]\}$ is an ideal of $\mathbb{R}[x, y]$. However, $U \cdot V = \{(xp_1 + yq_1) \cdot (xp_2 + yq_2) : p_1, p_2, q_1, q_2 \in \mathbb{R}[x, y]\}$ is not a subring and therefore not an ideal. Notice that x^2 and y^2 are in $U \cdot V$, but $x^2 + y^2$ is not in $U \cdot V$, because it cannot be factored into the product of polynomials of the form $xp + yq$ where p and q are in $\mathbb{R}[x, y]$.

III: The intersection of two subrings is always a subring, so we are safe in that respect. If w is in $U \cap V$, then w is in U and V. Because U and V are ideals, rw and wr are in U and V, which implies they are in $U \cap V$.

We select (D). ∎

Question 1.51. ——————————————————————————
We can immediately see that the second column adds nothing to the column space, because it is -1 times the first column. Hence, we need only find the column space of

$$\begin{pmatrix} 1 & 2 & -3 \\ -1 & -3 & 2 \\ 2 & 5 & -5 \end{pmatrix}.$$

We will row reduce the matrix to reduced row echelon form to find a basis for the column space. This yields

$$\begin{pmatrix} 1 & 0 & -5 \\ 0 & 1 & 1 \\ 0 & 0 & 0 \end{pmatrix}.$$

We conclude

$$\begin{pmatrix} 1 \\ -1 \\ 2 \end{pmatrix} \quad \text{and} \quad \begin{pmatrix} 2 \\ -3 \\ 5 \end{pmatrix}$$

form a basis for the column space, since there are pivots in the first and second column of the reduced row echelon form of our matrix.

Let's go through our candidate bases because we can exclude a few. We know the dimension of our column space is two, which means (B) is out. The basis in option (C) is not orthogonal, so we eliminate it as a possibility. The basis in option (D) is not normal, which allows us to exclude it from consideration. We can safely conclude that either (A) or (E) is correct.

Option (E) looks like a more viable basis than (A), so we will modify our basis to try to make it look like (D). Notice that there is no entry in the last row of the second vector in (E), and all of its entries are positive. Let's build a vector in the column space with these properties:

$$5 \begin{pmatrix} 1 \\ -1 \\ 2 \end{pmatrix} - 2 \begin{pmatrix} 2 \\ -3 \\ 5 \end{pmatrix} = \begin{pmatrix} 1 \\ 1 \\ 0 \end{pmatrix}.$$

It is not hard to see that our constructed vector is normal to

$$\begin{pmatrix} 1 \\ -1 \\ 2 \end{pmatrix}.$$

As a result, we will normalize the above vector and the one we constructed. This yields

$$\frac{1}{\sqrt{6}} \begin{pmatrix} 1 \\ -1 \\ 2 \end{pmatrix} = \begin{pmatrix} 1/\sqrt{6} \\ -1/\sqrt{6} \\ 2/\sqrt{6} \end{pmatrix} \quad \text{and} \quad \frac{1}{\sqrt{2}} \begin{pmatrix} 1 \\ 1 \\ 0 \end{pmatrix} = \begin{pmatrix} 1/\sqrt{2} \\ 1/\sqrt{2} \\ 0 \end{pmatrix}.$$

We have found an orthonormal basis, and it is the same as (E). ∎

Question 1.52. ──────────────────────────────
The first professor to receive their assignments could be assigned two classes in $_{20}C_2 = 20 \cdot 19/2$ different ways. Similarly, the second professor to be assigned courses could be assigned in $_{18}C_2 = 18 \cdot 17/2$ ways. Generally, the n-th professor could be assigned two classes in $_{(22-2n)}C_2 = (22 - 2n)(21 - 2n)/2$ different ways. It follows that there are

$$\left(\frac{20 \cdot 19}{2}\right) \left(\frac{18 \cdot 17}{2}\right) \cdots \left(\frac{4 \cdot 3}{2}\right) \left(\frac{2 \cdot 1}{2}\right) = \frac{20!}{2^{20}}$$

ways for the professors to be assigned classes. We conclude that (A) is correct. ∎

Question 1.53. ──────────────────────────────
This is an application of the *Fundamental theorem of Calculus,* several *integration properties,* and the product rule which is one of our *derivative rules.* We have

$$g(x) = \int_0^x f(y)(y - x) \, dy = \int_0^x y f(y) \, dy - x \int_0^x f(y) \, dy.$$

It follows that

$$g'(x) = x f(x) - \int_0^x f(y) \, dy - x f(x) = - \int_0^x f(y) \, dy.$$

So,

$$g''(x) = -f(x) \quad \text{and} \quad g'''(x) = -f'(x).$$

We conclude that f need only be continuously differentiable once, and we select (A). ∎

Question 1.54. ──────────────────────────────
Since all points (x, y) in $[0, 3] \times [0, 4]$ are equally as likely, the probability that $x < y$ is the ratio of the areas of $\{(x, y) \in [0, 3] \times [0, 4] :$

36

$x < y\}$ and $[0,3] \times [0,4]$.

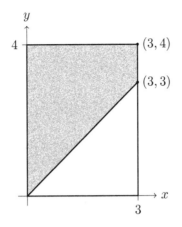

Hence,

$$P(x < y) = \frac{3(4+1)/2}{3(4)} = \frac{15}{24} = \frac{5}{8}.$$

Fill in (C) and continue! ∎

Question 1.55. ─────────────────────────────
We have

$$\int_0^\infty \frac{e^{ax} - e^{bx}}{(1+e^{ax})(1+e^{bx})} \, dx = \lim_{t \to \infty} \int_0^t \frac{1 + e^{ax} - (1+e^{bx})}{(1+e^{ax})(1+e^{bx})} \, dx$$

$$= \lim_{t \to \infty} \int_0^t \frac{1 + e^{ax}}{(1+e^{ax})(1+e^{bx})}$$

$$- \frac{1 + e^{bx}}{(1+e^{ax})(1+e^{bx})} \, dx$$

$$= \lim_{t \to \infty} \left(\int_0^t \frac{dx}{1+e^{bx}} - \int_0^t \frac{dx}{1+e^{ax}} \right)$$

Let $u := e^{bx}$ which implies $du = be^{bx} \, dx = bu \, dx$, and let $v := e^{ax}$

which implies $dv = ae^{ax}\, dx = av\, dx$. It follows that

$$\lim_{t \to \infty} \left(\int_0^t \frac{dx}{1 + e^{bx}} - \int_0^t \frac{dx}{1 + e^{ax}} \right)$$

$$= \lim_{t \to \infty} \left(\frac{1}{b} \int_{x=0}^t \frac{du}{u(u+1)} - \frac{1}{a} \int_{x=0}^t \frac{dv}{v(v+1)} \right)$$

$$= \lim_{t \to \infty} \left(\frac{1}{b} \int_{u=1}^{e^{bt}} \frac{du}{u(u+1)} - \frac{1}{a} \int_{v=1}^{e^{at}} \frac{dv}{v(v+1)} \right)$$

We need to break up the rational expressions in both integrands. Using *partial fraction decomposition*, we know that there are values of A and B such that

$$\frac{1}{w(w+1)} = \frac{A}{w} + \frac{B}{w+1}.$$

Multiplying both sides by $w(w+1)$ yields

$$1 = A(w+1) + Bw.$$

By equating coefficients or by selecting arbitrary values of w, we see $A = 1$ and $B = -1$. So,

$$\lim_{t \to \infty} \left(\frac{1}{b} \int_{u=1}^{e^{bt}} \frac{du}{u(u+1)} - \frac{1}{a} \int_{v=1}^{e^{at}} \frac{dv}{v(v+1)} \right)$$

$$= \lim_{t \to \infty} \left(\frac{1}{b} \int_1^{e^{bt}} \frac{1}{u} - \frac{1}{u+1}\, du - \frac{1}{a} \int_1^{e^{at}} \frac{1}{v} - \frac{1}{v+1}\, dv \right)$$

$$= \lim_{t \to \infty} \left(\frac{1}{b} \Big[\log u - \log(u+1) \Big]_1^{e^{bt}} - \frac{1}{a} \Big[\log v - \log(v+1) \Big]_1^{e^{at}} \right)$$

$$= \lim_{t \to \infty} \left(\frac{1}{b} \log \left(\frac{e^{bt}}{e^{bt}+1} \right) - \frac{1}{b} \log \left(\frac{1}{2} \right) - \frac{1}{a} \log \left(\frac{e^{at}}{e^{at}+1} \right) \right.$$

$$\left. + \frac{1}{a} \log \left(\frac{1}{2} \right) \right)$$

$$= \frac{1}{b} \log 1 + \frac{1}{b} \log 2 - \frac{1}{a} \log 1 - \frac{1}{a} \log 2$$

$$= \frac{a-b}{ab} \log 2.$$

The answer must be (E).

Note: a list of *logarithm properties* is located in the glossary. Also, if you feel that the above computation is too intensive for the GRE, the following two suggestions may be of utility: (1) You can choose values for a and b and compute the easier corresponding integrals. (2) The two integrals are nearly identical, so you can compute

$$\int \frac{dw}{w(w+1)}$$

and then insert the result where needed. ∎

Question 1.56.

Statement I is true. Because $\log 1 = 0 < 2\sqrt{1} = 2$ and

$$\frac{d}{dx}\left(\log x\right) = \frac{1}{x} \leq \frac{d}{dx}\left(2\sqrt{x}\right) = \frac{1}{\sqrt{x}}$$

for $x \geq 1$, we can conclude $\log x \leq 2\sqrt{x}$ for $x \geq 1$, because $2\sqrt{x}$ starts out larger and grows faster.

Statement II is false. One of the *summation formulas* from Calculus states that

$$\sum_{k=1}^{n} k^2 = \frac{n(n+1)(2n+1)}{6}.$$

Since the sum is equal to a polynomial of degree three with a positive leading coefficient, it will always overtake Cn^2, regardless of C, for sufficiently large n.

Statement III is true. Recall that the *Maclaurin series formula* for $f(x) := \sin x$ is

$$f(x) = x - \frac{x^3}{3!} + \frac{x^5}{5!} - \frac{x^7}{7!} + \ldots.$$

Furthermore, since $f(0) = 0$ and $f''(0) = 0$,

$$x = 0 + x + 0x^2 = \sum_{k=0}^{2} \frac{f^{(k)}(0)x^k}{k!}$$

39

qualifies as a second degree Taylor polynomial centered at 0. *Taylor's theorem* provides an error bound for this approximation. Let I be the open interval with endpoints x and 0. Then

$$\left| \sin x - x \right| \leq \sup_{t \in I} \left| f'''(t) \right| \frac{|x|^3}{3!}$$

$$= \sup_{t \in I} \left| -\sin t \right| \frac{|x|^3}{6}$$

$$\leq \frac{|x|^3}{6}.$$

Hence, the solution is (D). ∎

Question 1.57.
Statement I is true. We have $\lim_{n \to \infty} x_n = 0$ because

$$0 < x_n < \frac{1}{n} \quad \text{and} \quad \lim_{n \to \infty} 0 = 0 \leq \lim_{n \to \infty} x_n \leq \lim_{n \to \infty} \frac{1}{n} = 0.$$

Statement II is false. Consider

$$x_n := \frac{1}{n+1} \quad \text{and} \quad f(x) := \frac{1}{x}.$$

The function f is continuous and real-valued on the open interval $(0, 1)$, but

$$f(x_n) = n + 1 \to \infty \quad \text{as} \quad n \to \infty.$$

Because $\mathbb{R}$ is complete, a sequence converges whenever it is Cauchy. Since $\{f(x_n)\}_{n=1}^{\infty}$ diverges, it cannot be Cauchy.

Statement III is true. Recall the definition of *uniform continuity*:

Consider the metric spaces (X, ρ) and (Y, σ). A function $f : X \to Y$ is uniformly continuous on $U \subseteq X$ if and only if for all $\varepsilon > 0$ there is a $\delta > 0$ such that

$$\sigma\left(f(x_1), f(x_2)\right) < \varepsilon \quad \text{whenever} \quad \rho(x_1, x_2) < \delta,$$

for all x_1 and x_2 in U.

Within the context of this problem, this means that for all $\varepsilon > 0$ there exists a $\delta > 0$ such that, for x and y in the open interval $(0, 1)$,

$$|g(x) - g(y)| < \varepsilon \quad \text{whenever} \quad |x - y| < \delta.$$

From statement I, we know that x_n converges. So, for all $\eta > 0$ there exists a real number N such that

$$|x_m - x_n| < \eta \quad \text{whenever} \quad m, n > N.$$

When we pick an ε, let η equal the corresponding δ. Hence, for all $\varepsilon > 0$ there exists an N such that

$$|g(x_m) - g(x_n)| < \varepsilon \quad \text{whenever} \quad m, n > N.$$

Thus, $\{g(x_n)\}_{n=1}^{\infty}$ is a Cauchy sequence. All Cauchy sequences converge within the set of real numbers. The conclusion follows.

We are ready to select (C) and move on. ∎

Question 1.58.

The formula for the *arc length* of a parametric equation whose graph is contained within $\mathbb{R}^2$ is assumed knowledge. Our parametric equation is in $\mathbb{R}^3$, which makes finding its arc length more difficult.

Suppose that ΔL_i is the change in arc length from $\theta = \theta_{i-1}$ to θ_i. Let us find a formula for a small change of arc length ΔL_i in terms of the other variables, and then formulate the total length as the limit of a Riemann sum of ΔL_i's.

Let $\Delta x_i = x(\theta_i) - x(\theta_{i-1})$, $\Delta y_i = y(\theta_i) - y(\theta_{i-1})$, and $\Delta z_i = z(\theta_i) - z(\theta_{i-1})$. Because of the Euclidian metric, ΔL_i equals the square root of the sum of the squares of changes in each variable, i.e.

$$\Delta L_i = \sqrt{(\Delta x_i)^2 + (\Delta y_i)^2 + (\Delta z_i)^2}.$$

If follows that

$$\Delta L_i = \sqrt{\left(\frac{\Delta x_i}{\Delta \theta_i} \cdot \Delta \theta_i\right)^2 + \left(\frac{\Delta y_i}{\Delta \theta_i} \cdot \Delta \theta_i\right)^2 + \left(\frac{\Delta z_i}{\Delta \theta_i} \cdot \Delta \theta_i\right)^2}$$

$$= \sqrt{\left(\frac{\Delta x_i}{\Delta \theta_i}\right)^2 + \left(\frac{\Delta y_i}{\Delta \theta_i}\right)^2 + \left(\frac{\Delta z_i}{\Delta \theta_i}\right)^2} \, \Delta \theta_i,$$

where $\Delta\theta_i = \theta_i - \theta_{i-1}$.

Suppose θ goes from α to β. Consider the partition of the interval $\{\theta_i\}_{i=0}^n$ such that $\theta_i = (\beta - \alpha)i/n$. Notice $\sum_{i=1}^n \Delta L_i \approx L$, where L is the length of the arc from $\theta = \alpha$ to $\theta = \beta$. Furthermore, as $n \to \infty$, we have $\sum_{i=1}^n \Delta L_i \to L$ and

$$\sum_{i=1}^n \Delta L_i = \sum_{i=1}^n \sqrt{\left(\frac{\Delta x_i}{\Delta\theta_i}\right)^2 + \left(\frac{\Delta y_i}{\Delta\theta_i}\right)^2 + \left(\frac{\Delta z_i}{\Delta\theta_i}\right)^2} \, \Delta\theta_i$$

$$\longrightarrow \int_\alpha^\beta \sqrt{\left(\frac{dx}{d\theta}\right)^2 + \left(\frac{dy}{d\theta}\right)^2 + \left(\frac{dz}{d\theta}\right)^2} \, d\theta.$$

We conclude that

$$L = \int_\alpha^\beta \sqrt{\left(\frac{dx}{d\theta}\right)^2 + \left(\frac{dy}{d\theta}\right)^2 + \left(\frac{dz}{d\theta}\right)^2} \, d\theta.$$

We are ready to find a formula for $L(\theta)$, which is defined to be the arc length from θ to the point $(5, 0, 0)$. Let's consider the bounds of integration. Clearly, the lower bound of integration is the variable θ. Since $(5\cos\theta, 5\sin\theta, \theta) = (5, 0, 0)$ implies $\theta = 0$, the upper bound is $\theta = 0$. We introduce the dummy variable t within the integrand to avoid confusion between the bounds of integration, and the variable of integration. Hence,

$$L(\theta) = \int_\theta^0 \sqrt{(-5\sin t)^2 + (5\cos t)^2 + (1)^2} \, dt$$

$$= \int_\theta^0 \sqrt{25\sin^2 t + 25\cos^2 t + 1} \, dt$$

$$= \int_\theta^0 \sqrt{25 + 1} \, dt$$

$$= \int_\theta^0 \sqrt{26} \, dt$$

$$= -\theta\sqrt{26}.$$

So, $L(\theta_0) = 26$ implies $\theta_0 = -\sqrt{26}$. It follows that

$$x(\theta_0) = 5\cos\left(-\sqrt{26}\right), \quad y(\theta_0) = 5\sin\left(-\sqrt{26}\right), \quad \text{and} \quad z(\theta_0) = -\sqrt{26}.$$

Therefore,

$$D(\theta_0) = D\left(-\sqrt{26}\right)$$

$$= \sqrt{\left(5\cos\left(-\sqrt{26}\right) - 0\right)^2 + \left(5\sin\left(-\sqrt{26}\right) - 0\right)^2 + \left(-\sqrt{26} - 0\right)^2}$$

$$= \sqrt{25\cos^2\left(-\sqrt{26}\right) + 25\sin^2\left(-\sqrt{26}\right) + 26}$$

$$= \sqrt{25 + 26}$$

$$= \sqrt{51}.$$

We select (B). A list of *Pythagorean identities* is given in the glossary. ■

Question 1.59. ────────────────────────────────

We will go through our options. Some *determinant properties* are given in the glossary.

Option (A) is enough to conclude that A is invertible, because

$$\det(-A) = (-1)^3 \det(A) = -\det(A) \neq 0$$

implies $\det(A) \neq 0$.

Option (B) implies that A is invertible. This is due to the fact that

$$\det(A^k) = \left(\det(A)\right)^k \neq 0,$$

and by taking the k-th root of both sides, we see $\det(A) \neq 0$.

Option (C) is enough to conclude that A is invertible. We note the vector v being in the null space of A implies that either v is an eigenvector with an eigenvalue of 0 or $v = 0$, so if A has no eigenvectors or all of its eigenvectors have eigenvalues other than 0, A is invertible. Suppose v is an eigenvector of A with eigenvalue λ; if no such v exists, we are done. We want to show that λ cannot equal 0. The vector v is also an eigenvector of $I - A$ with eigenvalue $1 - \lambda$, because

$$(I - A)v = Iv - Av = v - \lambda v = (1 - \lambda)v.$$

It follows that
$$(I - A)^k \boldsymbol{v} = (1 - \lambda)^k \boldsymbol{v} = \boldsymbol{0}.$$

Since the eigenvector $\boldsymbol{v} \neq \boldsymbol{0}$, we have
$$(1 - \lambda)^k = 0 \quad \text{implies} \quad \lambda = 1 \neq 0.$$

We conclude A is invertible.

Option (D) is enough to conclude that A is invertible, due to the *Rank-nullity theorem*. It says

> Suppose V is a finite dimensional vector space and let $T : V \to W$ be a linear map. Then
> $$\text{nullity}(T) + \text{rank}(T) = \dim(V)$$

For us, $\text{nullity}(T) + \text{rank}(T) = 3$. Since $\{A\boldsymbol{v} : \boldsymbol{v} \in \mathbb{R}^3\} = \text{range}(A) = \mathbb{R}^3$, we know that the rank is three. This implies that the nullity is zero, which is equivalent to A being invertible.

By the process of elimination, the solution must be (E). Let's construct a counterexample. Let
$$\boldsymbol{v}_1 := \begin{pmatrix} 1 \\ 0 \\ 0 \end{pmatrix}, \quad \boldsymbol{v}_2 := \begin{pmatrix} 0 \\ 1 \\ 0 \end{pmatrix}, \quad \text{and} \quad \boldsymbol{v}_3 := \begin{pmatrix} 0 \\ 0 \\ 1 \end{pmatrix}.$$

Further, suppose
$$A := \begin{pmatrix} 1 & 1 & 1 \\ 0 & 0 & 0 \\ 0 & 0 & 0 \end{pmatrix}.$$

It is clear that $\boldsymbol{v}_1$, $\boldsymbol{v}_2$, and $\boldsymbol{v}_3$ are linearly independent, and $A\boldsymbol{v}_i \neq \boldsymbol{0}$ for each i. However, A is not invertible. ∎

Question 1.60.

The correct answer is (D), which says $\lim_{|x| \to \infty} |f(x)| = \infty$. We will consider each direction.

Suppose for any large $\varepsilon > 0$, there exists a $\delta > 0$ such that
$$|f(x) - f(1)| \geq \varepsilon \quad \text{whenever} \quad |x - 1| \geq \delta.$$

This implies $\lim_{|x| \to \infty} |f(x)| = \infty$, because we are guaranteed that we can make the distance between $f(x)$ and $f(1)$ arbitrarily large via selecting any x sufficiently far from 1.

The other direction is a little less clear. But let's prove this way works too. Suppose $\lim_{|x| \to \infty} |f(x)| = \infty$. Then for all $\eta > 0$, there exists an $N > 0$ such that

$$|f(x)| \geq \eta \quad \text{whenever} \quad |x| \geq N.$$

Pick an $\varepsilon > 0$. Let $\eta = \varepsilon + |f(1)|$. There exists an $N > 0$ such that $|f(x)| \geq \varepsilon + |f(1)|$ whenever $|x| \geq N$. Due to the triangle inequality,

$$|f(x) - f(1)| + |f(1)| \geq |f(x)| \geq \varepsilon + |f(1)|.$$

It follows that $|f(x) - f(1)| \geq \varepsilon$.

If $|x| \geq N$, then

$$x \geq N \quad \text{or} \quad x \leq -N.$$

This is equivalent to

$$x - 1 \geq N - 1 \quad \text{or} \quad x - 1 \leq -(N + 1).$$

Since

$$x - 1 \geq N + 1 \quad \text{implies} \quad x - 1 \geq N - 1$$

we have $|x| \geq N$ whenever $|x - 1| \geq N + 1$. So, there exists a $\delta > 0$ such that

$$|f(x) - f(1)| \geq \varepsilon \quad \text{whenever} \quad |x - 1| \geq \delta,$$

specifically $\delta = N + 1$.

Note: On the actual GRE proofs are not required, and can even be counter-productive because they tend to take up more time. Instead, we advise drawing pictures that illustrate the phenomenon above. We omitted such pictures from this text because it would make the presentation highly heterodox, and explaining the meaning and choice of our arbitrary notation and pictures would require a lot of space. ∎

Question 1.61. ───────────────────────────────

Let's solve this mixing problem via the usual differential equation techniques. We omit units during calculations for convenience. Suppose that y is the amount of salt in the tank after t minutes. We are given that $y(0) = 3$. Because the rate of change of salt with respect to time is the rate salt comes into the tank minus the rate it goes out,

$$\frac{dy}{dt} = 4(0.02) - 4\left(\frac{y}{100}\right) = \frac{2-y}{25}.$$

This implies

$$\frac{1}{y-2}\frac{dy}{dt} = -\frac{1}{25}$$

$$\Rightarrow \quad \int \frac{dy}{y-2} = -\frac{1}{25}\int dt$$

$$\Rightarrow \quad \log|y-2| = -\frac{t}{25} + C$$

$$\Rightarrow \quad y - 2 = \pm e^C \cdot e^{-t/25}$$

$$\Rightarrow \quad y = 2 + Ke^{-t/25},$$

where $K = \pm e^C$. It follows that

$$y(0) = 2 + Ke^0 = 2 + K = 3 \quad \text{implies} \quad K = 1.$$

Thus,

$$y(100) = 2 + e^{-4}.$$

Option (E) is correct. ∎

Question 1.62. ———————————————————————

Let's go through why S is neither open nor closed. Every open ball in $[0,1] \times [0,1]$ contains points in $\mathbb{Q} \times \mathbb{Q}$. As such, S has no interior points, which implies it is not open. The set S does not contain all of its limit points so it cannot be closed, e.g. the point $(1/2, 1/2)$ is a limit point of S not contained within S.

Since S is not closed, it is not *compact*. This is due to the *Heine-Borel theorem* which says a subset of $\mathbb{R}^n$, for any natural number n, is compact if and only if it is closed and bounded.

The set S is connected. For any a and b in $[0,1] \setminus \mathbb{Q}$, S contains the paths $\{(a,t) : 0 \le t \le 1\}$ and $\{(t,b) : 0 \le t \le 1\}$. As a result, it is not difficult to find a path between two arbitrary points in S. It follows that S is path connected, which implies that it is connected because path connectivity is a stronger claim. Obviously, if S is connected, we can safely rule out it being completely disconnected. It is time to select (C). ∎

Question 1.63. ———————————————————————

The answer is (E). It is easy enough to falsify the others with counterexamples.

For (A), (B), (C), and (D), consider $A = (1,2)$ and $B = (-2,-1)$. Then

- $\sup(A)\sup(B) = -2$,

- $\sup(A)\inf(B) = -4$,

- $\max\{\sup(A)\sup(B), \inf(A)\inf(B)\} = \max\{-2,-2\} = -2$,

- $\max\{\sup(A)\sup(B), \sup(A)\inf(B)\} = \max\{-2,-4\} = -2$,

but $\sup(A \cdot B) = -1$. ∎

Question 1.64. ────────────────────────────

We will use the *divergence theorem*. It says:

> Suppose the closed surface S with outward orientation is the boundary of a solid E, and $\boldsymbol{F}$ is a vector field with continuous first order partial derivatives. Then the *flux* of $\boldsymbol{F}$ through S is
>
> $$\oiint_S \boldsymbol{F} \cdot d\boldsymbol{S} = \iiint_E \text{div}(\boldsymbol{F})\, dV,$$
>
> where
>
> $$\text{div}(\boldsymbol{F}) := \left(\frac{\partial}{\partial x}, \frac{\partial}{\partial y}, \frac{\partial}{\partial z} \right) \cdot \boldsymbol{F}.$$

Let S be the surface described by $z = \sqrt{1 - x^2 - y^2}$. Unfortunately, S is not a closed surface. To avoid a direction computation of the flux through S, we consider the flux though the closed surface $S \cup T$, where

$$T := \{(x, y, z) \in \mathbb{R}^3 : x^2 + y^2 \leq 1,\ z = 0\}.$$

Since T is contained within the plane $z = 0$, it will be easier to compute the flux of $\boldsymbol{F}$ through T directly than it would be to compute the flux through S directly.

It is not too tough to see that $S \cup T$ forms the boundary of

$$E := \{(x, y, z) \in \mathbb{R}^3 : x^2 + y^2 + z^2 \leq 1,\ z \geq 0\}.$$

As a result, the divergence theorem tells us

$$\oiint_S \boldsymbol{F} \cdot d\boldsymbol{S} + \oiint_T \boldsymbol{F} \cdot d\boldsymbol{S} = \oiint_{S \cup T} \boldsymbol{F} \cdot d\boldsymbol{S} = \iiint_E \text{div}(\boldsymbol{F})\, dV.$$

From here, the calculation is fairly straightforward. Notice that $z = \sqrt{1 - x^2 - y^2}$ is the upper half of a sphere of radius one, which implies that its volume is

$$\frac{1}{2} \left(\frac{4}{3} \pi (1)^3 \right) = \frac{2\pi}{3}.$$

48

Then the flux of $\boldsymbol{F}$ through $S \cup T$ is

$$
\iiint\limits_{E} \mathrm{div}(\boldsymbol{F})\ dV = \iiint\limits_{E} \frac{\partial}{\partial x}\left(x\right) + \frac{\partial}{\partial y}\left(y\right) + \frac{\partial}{\partial z}\left(z\right)\ dV
$$

$$
= \iiint\limits_{E} 3\ dV
$$

$$
= 3\left(\frac{2\pi}{3}\right)
$$

$$
= 2\pi.
$$

To find the flux of $\boldsymbol{F}$ through S, we compute the flux though T and subtract this result from the flux through $S \cup T$. Recall

$$
\oiint\limits_{T} \boldsymbol{F} \cdot d\boldsymbol{S} = \oiint\limits_{T} \boldsymbol{F} \cdot \boldsymbol{n}\ dS,
$$

where $\boldsymbol{n}$ is normal to T. Since T has outward orientation relative to E, and T lies on the plane $z = 0$, $\boldsymbol{n} = \left(0, 0, -1\right)$. Hence,

$$
\oiint\limits_{T} \boldsymbol{F} \cdot \boldsymbol{n}\ dS = \oiint\limits_{T} \left(x, y, 0\right) \cdot \left(0, 0, -1\right)\ dS
$$

$$
= \oiint\limits_{T} 0\ dS
$$

$$
= 0.
$$

We conclude

$$
\oiint\limits_{S} \boldsymbol{F} \cdot d\boldsymbol{S} = 2\pi - 0 = 2\pi.
$$

Fill in the bubble for (E).   ■

Question 1.65. ────────────────────────────

Recall the *necessary and sufficient* condition for a function to be *analytic*:

> The function $f(z) = u(x,y) + iv(x,y)$ is analytic if and only if
> $$\frac{\partial u}{\partial x} = \frac{\partial v}{\partial y} \quad \text{and} \quad \frac{\partial u}{\partial y} = -\frac{\partial v}{\partial x}.$$

It follows that

$$g_y(x,y) = e^x \sin y \quad \text{and} \quad g_x(x,y) = -e^x \cos y.$$

Using "partial integration" (i.e. treating the variables that we are not integrating with respect to as constants during integration), we can see that

$$
\begin{aligned}
g(x,y) &= \int g_y(x,y)\,dy & \text{and} && g(x,y) &= \int g_x(x,y)\,dx \\
&= \int e^x \sin y\,dy & && &= \int -e^x \cos y\,dx \\
&= -e^x \cos y + h_1(x) & && &= -e^x \cos y + h_2(y).
\end{aligned}
$$

It follows that $h_1(x) = h_2(y)$ is constant, because there are no terms of only y in the first integral and no terms of only x in the second. Hence,

$$g(3,2) - g(1,2) = -e^3 \cos 2 + e^1 \cos 2 = (e - e^3)\cos 2.$$

The solution must be (E). ∎

Question 1.66. ───────────────────────────────

Recall that m is a unit of $\mathbb{Z}_n$ if and only if the greatest common factor of m and n is 1. Since 17 is a prime number, every non-zero element of $\mathbb{Z}_{17}$ is a unit. It follows that the order of $\mathbb{Z}_{17}^{\times}$ is 16.

Lagrange's theorem says that the order of a subgroup must divide the order of the entire group. It follows that our contenders, 5, 8, and 16, could only generate cyclic subgroups of order 1, 2, 4, 8, or 16. We can immediately exclude 1 from being the order of any of our subgroups because it is clear that none of our contenders could be the multiplicative identity.

Let's consider 5. We will compute 5 raised to each of the possible orders:

$$5^2 \equiv 25 \qquad\qquad 5^4 \equiv 8^2 \qquad\qquad 5^8 \equiv 13^2$$
$$\equiv 8 \quad (\mathrm{mod}\ 17), \qquad \equiv 64 \qquad\qquad \equiv 169$$
$$\equiv 13 \quad (\mathrm{mod}\ 17), \qquad \equiv 16 \quad (\mathrm{mod}\ 17),$$

and

$$5^{16} \equiv 16^2$$
$$\equiv 256$$
$$\equiv 1 \quad (\mathrm{mod}\ 17).$$

We can conclude that 5 generates a cyclic subgroup of order 16, which implies it generates $\mathbb{Z}_{17}^{\times}$.

We have also proven that 8 and 16 are not generators, because

$$5^2 \equiv 8 \quad (\mathrm{mod}\ 17) \quad \text{implies} \quad 5^{16} \equiv 8^8 \equiv 1 \quad (\mathrm{mod}\ 17),$$

which means 8 generates a cyclic subgroup of order 8. Similarly,

$$5^8 \equiv 16 \quad (\mathrm{mod}\ 17) \quad \text{implies} \quad 5^{16} \equiv 16^2 \equiv 1 \quad (\mathrm{mod}\ 17),$$

which means that 16 generates of cyclic subgroup of order 2. Thus, we select (B). ■

Chapter 2

GR0568 Solutions

Suppose x and y are differentiable functions of a parameter t. Then the *arc length* of the curve described by x and y between the points corresponding to $t = a$ and $t = b$ is

$$s = \int_a^b \sqrt{\left(\frac{dx}{dt}\right)^2 + \left(\frac{dy}{dt}\right)^2}\, dt.$$

Let's find the pieces:

$$x = \cos t \quad \text{implies} \quad \frac{dx}{dt} = -\sin t$$

and

$$y = \sin t \quad \text{implies} \quad \frac{dy}{dt} = \cos t.$$

Since t goes from 0 to π, we have

$$
\begin{aligned}
s &= \int_0^\pi \sqrt{\left(-\sin t\right)^2 + \left(\cos t\right)^2}\, dt \\
&= \int_0^\pi \sqrt{\sin^2 t + \cos^2 t}\ dt \\
&= \int_0^\pi 1\ dt \\
&= \pi.
\end{aligned}
$$

We conclude that the answer is (B). ∎

Question 2.2.

To find a tangent line of a curve, we need a point on the curve and the slope at that point. First, we will find the point. If $x = 0$, then $y = 0 + e^0 = 1$. Hence, the graph contains $(0, 1)$. Next, we will find the slope. The derivative $y' = 1 + e^x$ gives the slope of the curve at x. It follows that the slope at $x = 0$ is $y' = 1 + e^0 = 2$. Thus, the equation of the tangent line is $y = 2x + 1$. Pick (E) and continue. A list of useful *derivatives* is located in the glossary. ∎

Question 2.3.

Since $V \cap W \subseteq V$,

$$0 \le \dim(V \cap W) \le \dim(V) \quad \text{implies} \quad 0 \le \dim(V \cap W) \le 2.$$

We have shown that $V \cap W$ cannot have dimension greater than 2. To see that it is possible for $V \cap W$ to have dimension 0, 1, or 2, suppose $V = \mathrm{span}\{(1,0,0,0),(0,1,0,0)\}$ and note that ...

- $W = \mathrm{span}\{(0,0,1,0),(0,0,0,1)\}$ implies $\dim(W \cap V) = 0$.
- $W = \mathrm{span}\{(0,1,0,0),(0,0,1,0)\}$ implies $\dim(W \cap V) = 1$.
- $W = \mathrm{span}\{(1,0,0,0),(0,1,0,0)\}$ implies $\dim(W \cap V) = 2$.

The correct answer must be (D). ∎

Question 2.4.

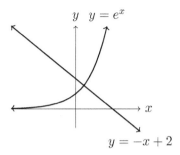

$$y \quad y = e^x$$

$$x$$

$$y = -x + 2$$

Since

$$e^x + x - 2 = 0 \quad \text{implies} \quad e^x = -x + 2,$$

we can determine the number of solutions of our equation by finding the number of times $y = e^x$ and $y = -x + 2$ intersect. Using basic graphing techniques, it's clear that there is exactly one point of intersection. It follows that $e^x + x - 2$ has only one zero.

We will show that our zero is in the interval $[0, 1]$ using the *Intermediate value theorem*. Let $f(x) := e^x + x - 2$. The function f satisfies the criteria for the intermediate value theorem because it is real-valued and continuous. Furthermore, notice

$$f(0) = -1 \quad \text{and} \quad f(1) = e - 1 \approx 1.7.$$

So, there must be a c in the interval $[0, 1]$ such that $f(c) = 0$. It follows that $k = 1$ and $n = 0$. Fill in the bubble for (B). ■

Question 2.5.

Since the coefficient in front of x^2 is 3 and the vertex of f is $(2, 0)$, $f(x) = 3(x - 2)^2$. Alternatively, we can find b:

$$f(2) = 2b + 24 = 0 \quad \text{implies} \quad b = -12.$$

Either way, it follows that

$$f(5) = 3(5 - 2)^2 = 3(9) = 27.$$

Therefore, (B) is correct. ■

Question 2.6. ―――――――――――――――――――――――――

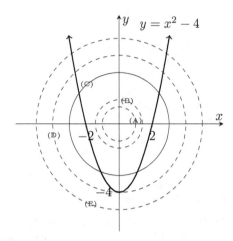

By drawing a picture, we see that there are at most four places where a circle centered at $(0,0)$ will intersect the parabola, and this optimal state is achieved when the radius is 3. Hence, we select (C).

Let's analyze this further, since we're not on the clock. Substituting $y + 4$ for x^2 in the equation $x^2 + y^2 = r^2$ gives

$$y + 4 + y^2 = r^2 \quad \text{implies} \quad y^2 + y + 4 - r^2 = 0.$$

Using the *discriminant* $1 - 4(4 - r^2) = 4r^2 - 15$, it follows that:

- If $r > \sqrt{15}/2$, two values of y satisfy $y^2 + y + 4 - r^2 = 0$.
- If $r = \sqrt{15}/2$, only $y = -1/2$ satisfies $y^2 + y + 4 - r^2 = 0$.
- If $r < \sqrt{15}/2$, no y will satisfy $y^2 + y + 4 - r^2 = 0$.

Via examination of the graph and a little algebra, we can make a few observations. For $r < 4$, each value of y which satisfies $y^2 + y + 4 - r^2 = 0$ corresponds to two intersections on the parabola, one with a negative x-value and one with a positive x-value. For $r = 4$, there will be a total of three intersections, $(-\sqrt{7}, 3)$, $(\sqrt{7}, 3)$, and $(0, -4)$; there is only one intersection corresponding to $y = -4$ because the circle is tangent to the parabola at $(0, -4)$. For $r > 4$, there will be a total of two intersections. In summery:

- If $r < \sqrt{15}/2$, the circle will never intersect the parabola.
- If $r = \sqrt{15}/2$, the circle will intersect the parabola at two points.
- If $\sqrt{15}/2 < r < 4$, the circle will intersect the parabola at four points.
- If $r = 4$, the circle will intersect the parabola at three points.
- If $r > 4$, the circle will intersect the parabola at two points.

■

Question 2.7. ────────────────────────────

It's clear $|x + 1| = \begin{cases} x + 1, & \text{if } x \geq -1 \\ -(x + 1), & \text{if } x < -1 \end{cases}$. So,

$$\int_{-3}^{3} |x + 1| \, dx = \int_{-3}^{-1} -(x + 1) \, dx + \int_{-1}^{3} x + 1 \, dx$$

$$= -\int_{-3}^{-1} x + 1 \, dx + \int_{-1}^{3} x + 1 \, dx$$

$$= -\left[\frac{x^2}{2} + x \right]_{-3}^{-1} + \frac{x^2}{2} + x \Big|_{-1}^{3}$$

$$= -\left(\frac{1}{2} - 1 \right) + \left(\frac{9}{2} - 3 \right) + \frac{9}{2} + 3 - \left(\frac{1}{2} - 1 \right)$$

$$= 10.$$

Thus, (C) is the answer.

■

Question 2.8. ————————————————————

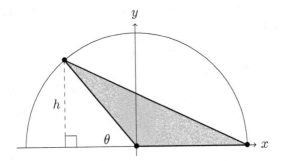

Without loss of generality, we can assume one side of our triangle is on the positive x-axis. Let h and θ be as shown in the picture. Due to symmetry, we only need to consider values of θ between 0 and 180°. In this interval, $h = \sin\theta$.

From geometry, we know the area A of our triangle is

$$A = \frac{1}{2} \cdot 1 \cdot h = \frac{\sin\theta}{2}.$$

The maximum value of $\sin\theta$, for θ between 0 and 180°, is 1, so the maximum value of A must be $1/2$. We conclude that (A) is correct. ■

Question 2.9. ————————————————————
Suppose that $0 \leq x \leq 1$. Since $0 \leq x^8 \leq x^4 \leq 1$,

$$\sqrt{1 - x^4} \leq \sqrt{1 - x^8} \leq 1 \leq \sqrt{1 + x^4}.$$

Indeed, the inequalities above are strict everywhere except $x = 0$ and 1. Therefore, basic *integration properties* tell us

$$\int_0^1 \sqrt{1 - x^4}\, dx < \int_0^1 \sqrt{1 - x^8}\, dx < 1 < \int_0^1 \sqrt{1 + x^4}\, dx.$$

Note that the integral inequalities are strict, since the integrands are only equal at a finite set of values. Fill in the bubble for (A). ■

Question 2.10. ────────────────────────────

This is a simple application of the *first derivative test.* Our critical numbers are 2 and 5. Let's make a table to see where g is increasing and decreasing:

Interval	$(-\infty, 2)$	$(2, 5)$	$(5, \infty)$
Test number	1	3	6
$g'(x)$	$g'(1) > 0$	$g'(3) < 0$	$g'(6) > 0$
g Increasing/Decreasing	Increasing	Decreasing	Increasing

Let's go through the ones that are false first. The number $g(1)$ is nothing special since g keeps increasing until 2. Neither $g(3)$ nor $g(4)$ is a relative extremum, since g is decreasing between 2 and 5. The value $g(5)$ is a relative minimum.

The value $g(2)$ must be the largest by the process of elimination. Indeed, the first derivative test tells us that the value $g(2)$ is a relative maximum. We select (B). ∎

Question 2.11. ────────────────────────────

It's not too hard to see that $1.5 \cdot 266 = 399$, which is approximately equal to the perfect square 400. Our strategy will be to modify $\sqrt{1.5}(266)^{3/2}$ so that only 399 is within the radical:

$$\sqrt{1.5}(266)^{3/2} = \sqrt{1.5 \cdot 266^3} = 266\sqrt{1.5 \cdot 266} = 266\sqrt{399}.$$

So,

$$\sqrt{1.5}(266)^{3/2} \approx 266\sqrt{400} = 266 \cdot 20 = 5,320.$$

This would be a good time to select (E) during testing. But we're not being timed (now), so let's see how much error we're talking about. From Calculus, we know

$$f(x + \Delta x) - f(x) \approx f'(x)\Delta x.$$

Define $f(x) := 266\sqrt{x}$. Then

$$f'(400) = \frac{133}{\sqrt{400}} = 6.65 \quad \text{and} \quad \Delta x = 399 - 400 = -1.$$

It follows that $f(399) - f(400) \approx -6.65$, which implies

$$f(399) \approx 5,320 - 6.65 = 5,313.35.$$

Using a calculator, we see that $f(399) = 5,313.34\ldots$. Thus, (E) gives us the closest approximation. ∎

Question 2.12.

It's clear A is of the form $\begin{pmatrix} a & b \\ b & a \end{pmatrix}$, where $a + b = k$. Thus,

$$A\begin{pmatrix} 1 \\ 0 \end{pmatrix} = \begin{pmatrix} a \\ b \end{pmatrix}, \quad A\begin{pmatrix} 0 \\ 1 \end{pmatrix} = \begin{pmatrix} b \\ a \end{pmatrix},$$

and

$$A\begin{pmatrix} 1 \\ 1 \end{pmatrix} = \begin{pmatrix} a+b \\ a+b \end{pmatrix} = \begin{pmatrix} k \\ k \end{pmatrix} = k\begin{pmatrix} 1 \\ 1 \end{pmatrix}.$$

We conclude that $\begin{pmatrix} 1 \\ 1 \end{pmatrix}$ is the only eigenvector listed, and we fill in the bubble for (C). ∎

Question 2.13.

Let the area in the yard be $A := \ell w$, where ℓ is the length and w is the width of the yard. By hypothesis, $\ell + 2w = x$. Using substitution, it follows that $A = (x - 2w)w = xw - 2w^2$. Hence, $dA/dw = x - 4w$. Letting $dA/dw = 0$ and solving for w yields $w = x/4$. Because this is a parabola with a negative coefficient in front of the w^2, this critical number maximizes A. Thus,

$$A = \left(x - \frac{2x}{4}\right)\frac{x}{4} = \frac{x^2}{8}$$

is the maximum area, so (B) is correct. ∎

Question 2.14. ───────────────────────────────────

This problem is equivalent to finding 7^{25} (mod 10). We can use exponent properties to simplify the expression:

$$7^{25} \equiv 7^{24} \cdot 7 \equiv 49^{12} \cdot 7 \equiv 9^{12} \cdot 7 \pmod{10}.$$

Another application of some of the same exponent properties completes the problem:

$$7^{25} \equiv 9^{12} \cdot 7 \equiv 81^6 \cdot 7 \equiv 1^6 \cdot 7 \equiv 7 \pmod{10}.$$

Pick (D) and continue to the next problem. ■

Question 2.15. ───────────────────────────────────

Let's go through the ones that are necessarily true first.

Option (A) must be true so we can eliminate it as a possibility. The *Heine-Borel theorem* says that a subset of $\mathbb{R}$ is closed and bounded if and only if it is *compact*. The closed interval $[-2, 3]$ is compact, and the image of a compact set under a continuous map is compact. Thus, f must be bounded.

We can jettison (B) because it is necessarily true. The function f is integrable over the closed interval $[-2, 3]$, because it is continuous over the interval $[-2, 3]$.

It cannot be (C) or (D) because they must be true too. Option (C) is the *Intermediate value theorem*, and (D) is the integral form of the *Mean value theorem*.

By the process of elimination, choice (E) must be the correct answer. It could be true or false, because

$$f'(0) := \lim_{h \to 0} \frac{f(h) - f(0)}{h}.$$

In other words, (E) is the claim that f is differentiable at 0. Since differentiability is a stronger claim than continuity, the limit does not need to exist. Consider the counterexample $f(x) = |x|$; f is not differentiable at 0, though it is continuous and real-valued on the interval $[-2, 3]$. ■

Question 2.16. ———————————————————————

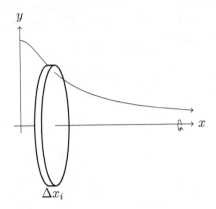

The first step is to find a formula for a slice of volume ΔV_i. At the point $(x_i, 1/\sqrt{1+(x_i)^2})$, the cross-section perpendicular to the xy-plane is a disk of radius $1/\sqrt{1+(x_i)^2}$, so its area must be

$$\pi \left(\frac{1}{\sqrt{1+(x_i)^2}} \right)^2 = \frac{\pi}{1+(x_i)^2}.$$

Multiplying by a small horizontal length $\Delta x_i = x_{i+1} - x_i$ gives us

$$\Delta V_i = \frac{\pi}{1+(x_i)^2} \, \Delta x_i.$$

Consider a partition $\{x_i\}_{i=0}^n$ of the interval $[0, b]$ such that $x_i = bi/n$. Notice that $\sum_{i=0}^n \Delta V_i$ is approximately equal to the volume of the solid generated by rotating the region bounded by the $x = 0$, $x = b$, $y = 0$, and $y = 1/\sqrt{1+x^2}$ about the x-axis. Furthermore, as $n \to \infty$, we have $\sum_{i=0}^n \Delta V_i$ approximates this volume more exactly and

$$\sum_{i=0}^n \Delta V_i = \sum_{i=0}^n \frac{\pi}{1+(x_i)^2} \, \Delta x_i \longrightarrow \int_0^b \frac{\pi}{1+x^2} \, dx.$$

Hence, the volume generated by the region corresponding to x in the interval $[0, b]$ is

$$\int_0^b \frac{\pi}{1+x^2} \, dx.$$

As $b \to \infty$, we see that the entire volume V is described via the equation

$$
\begin{aligned}
V &= \int_0^\infty \frac{\pi}{1 + x^2} \, dx \\
&= \pi \left[\text{Arctan } x \right]_0^\infty \\
&= \pi \left(\lim_{t \to \infty} \text{Arctan } t - \text{Arctan } 0 \right) \\
&= \pi \left(\frac{\pi}{2} - 0 \right) \\
&= \frac{\pi^2}{2}.
\end{aligned}
$$

Thus, (D) is correct.

We went through the reasoning behind the *disk method*. On the exam, it is not wise to go through the entire process due to time. However, an understanding of the reasoning behind the disk method is critical for mastery of it. ∎

Question 2.17. ———————————————————————

Descartes' rule of signs says:

> Suppose $f(x) = a_n x^n + a_{n-1} x^{n-1} + \ldots + a_1 x + a_0$. Then the number of positive zeros of f is equal to the number of sign changes of $f(x)$ or an even number fewer. Furthermore, the number of negative zeros of f is equal to the number of sign changes of $f(-x)$ or an even number fewer.

Since there is one sign change in $2x^5 + 8x - 7$, Descartes' rule of signs implies $2x^5 + 8x - 7$ has one positive zero. To find the number of negative zeros, consider $2(-x)^5 + 8(-x) - 7 = -2x^5 - 8x - 7$. There are no sign changes which implies there are no negative zeros. Thus, $2x^5 + 8x - 7$ has one real zero, which implies (B) is our winner. ∎

Question 2.18. ─────────────────────────────────

Recall that the nullity of T and the rank of T are defined to be the dimensions of the null space and the image, respectively. Since $\{v \in V : T(v) = \mathbf{0}\}$ is the definition of the null space, all we need to do is collect the pieces and apply the *Rank-nullity theorem*. The dimension of V is 6, and the dimension of W is 4. Since T is onto, the dimension of the range must be the same as the dimension of the codomain, i.e. the rank must be 4. It follows that $n + 4 = 6$, where n is the dimension of the null space. Thus, $n = 2$ and we pick (A). ∎

Question 2.19. ─────────────────────────────────

Elementary *integration properties* tell us that

$$\int_0^x f'(t)\,dt > \int_0^x g'(t)\,dt$$

because $f'(x) > g'(x)$ for $x > 0$. Using the *Fundamental theorem of Calculus*, we conclude

$$f(x) - f(0) > g(x) - g(0).$$

Fill in the bubble for (C). ∎

Question 2.20. ─────────────────────────────────

Recall that the real-valued function f is continuous at c if and only if

$$\lim_{x \to c} f(x) = f(c).$$

Let $\{q_n\}_{n=1}^{\infty}$ be a sequence of rational numbers such that $q_n \to c$ as $n \to \infty$, and let $\{x_n\}_{n=1}^{\infty}$ be a sequence of irrationals such that $x_n \to c$ as $n \to \infty$. Then

$$f(q_n) \to \frac{c}{2} \quad \text{and} \quad f(x_n) \to \frac{c}{3},$$

as $n \to \infty$. But $\lim_{x \to c} f(x)$ cannot equal two different values if f is continuous at c, so

$$\frac{c}{2} = \frac{c}{3} \quad \text{implies} \quad c = 0.$$

This means that 0 is the only possible value where f could be continuous and $\lim_{x \to 0} f(x) = 0$. We know $f(0) = 0/2 = 0$, so f is indeed continuous at 0. Therefore, f is discontinuous everywhere except 0 and (D) is the correct answer. ∎

Question 2.21. ───────────────────────────
The set $P_{12} \cap P_{20} = \{60\}$ is nonempty because $12 \cdot 5 = 20 \cdot 3$. So, the answer is (C).

Let's spend a bit of time thinking about the general rule. Suppose $P_m \cap P_n$ is nonempty and $m \neq n$. Then there must be primes p and q such that $m \cdot p = n \cdot q$. When this is the case, m and n share all but one prime factor; m has one more factor of q than n, and n has one more factor of p than m. In our case, 12 has one more factor of 3 than 20, and 20 has one more factor of 5 than 12. ∎

Question 2.22. ───────────────────────────
It's clear that I and II are subspaces, but III isn't because it's not closed under scalar addition (among other reasons). Suppose h is in

$$\{h : \ h \text{ is twice differentiable and } h''(x) = h(x) + 1 \text{ for all } x\}.$$

Then
$$h''(x) = h(x) + 1 \quad \text{implies} \quad h(x) = h''(x) - 1.$$

For r in $\mathbb{R}$,
$$rh(x) = rh''(x) + r \neq rh''(x) + 1$$

when $r \neq 1$. It is time to select (B).

In the previous editions, we checked the subspace axioms for I and II. Because this doesn't add much insight but does use a lot of paper, we will leave them out. Incredulous readers are invited to verify the axioms themselves or see our old verification at

rambotutoring.com/GR056822subspace.pdf

∎

65

Question 2.23.

Let's relabel to avoid confusion. Define

$$f(x) := 10x \quad \text{and} \quad g(x) := e^{bx}.$$

If f is tangent to g at $x = x_0$, then

$$f'(x_0) = g'(x_0) \quad \text{implies} \quad 10 = be^{bx_0}.$$

Solving for x_0 yields $x_0 = \log(10/b)/b$.

To be tangent, we need $f(x_0) = g(x_0)$. Let's evaluate f and g at $x_0 = \log(10/b)/b$:

$$f\left(\frac{\log(10/b)}{b}\right) = \frac{10\log(10/b)}{b}$$

and

$$g\left(\frac{\log(10/b)}{b}\right) = e^{\log(10/b)} = \frac{10}{b}.$$

It follows that

$$\frac{10\log(10/b)}{b} = \frac{10}{b} \quad \text{implies} \quad \log\left(\frac{10}{b}\right) = 1.$$

Using *logarithm properties* to change the equation to exponential form gives $10/b = e^1$. Therefore, $b = 10/e$. Pick (A)! ■

Question 2.24.

Let's try the direct approach:

$$h(x) = \int_0^{x^2} e^{x+t}dt = e^{x+t}\Big|_{t=0}^{x^2} = e^{x^2+x} - e^x.$$

Note that x is fixed with respect to t, so x behaves like a constant while integrating with respect to t.

Now to differentiate:

$$h'(x) = \frac{d}{dx}\left(e^{x^2+x} - e^x\right) = (2x+1)e^{x^2+x} - e^x.$$

We conclude $h'(1) = (2+1)e^{1+1} - e = 3e^2 - e$, and select (E). ■

Question 2.25. ─────────────────────────────

Let's see what a_{30} looks like:

$$a_{30} = \frac{31}{29} \cdot \frac{30}{28} \cdot \frac{29}{27} \cdot \frac{28}{26} \cdots \cdot \frac{6}{4} \cdot \frac{5}{3} \cdot \frac{4}{2} \cdot \frac{3}{1} \cdot 1.$$

So the numerator in the n-th factor will cancel with the denominator in $(n+2)$-th factor most of the time. When won't this happen? Well, the numerators in the twenty-ninth factor (30/28) and thirtieth factor (31/29) won't cancel, because there are no thirty-first and thirty-second factors. Furthermore, since there is no -1-th, no 0-th factor, and the rule is different for the first factor, the denominators in the first factor (1=1/1), the second factor (3/1), and the third factor (4/2) don't cancel. With our cancelation rules in mind, we see

$$a_{30} = \frac{31}{1} \cdot \frac{30}{1} \cdot \frac{1}{2} \cdot \frac{1}{1} \cdot 1 = (31)(15).$$

Choose (A) and continue! ■

Question 2.26. ─────────────────────────────

Recall the *second derivatives test* from third semester Calculus:

Suppose that the function $f : \mathbb{R}^2 \to \mathbb{R}$ has continuous second order partial derivatives in some $E \subseteq \mathbb{R}^2$. Suppose the point (a, b) in E is a critical point, i.e. $f_x(a, b) = 0$ and $f_y(a, b) = 0$. Define

$$H_f(x, y) := \det \begin{pmatrix} f_{xx}(x, y) & f_{xy}(x, y) \\ f_{yx}(x, y) & f_{yy}(x, y) \end{pmatrix}$$
$$= f_{xx}(x, y) f_{yy}(x, y) - [f_{xy}(x, y)]^2.$$

- If $f_{xx}(a, b) > 0$ and $H_f(a, b) > 0$, then $f(a, b)$ is a relative minimum.

- If $f_{xx}(a, b) < 0$ and $H_f(a, b) > 0$, then $f(a, b)$ is a relative maximum.

67

- If $H_f(a, b) < 0$, then (a, b) is a saddle point.
- If $H_f(a, b) = 0$, then the test gives no information.

Let's find our critical points. The partial derivative with respect to x and y are

$$f_x(x, y) = 2x - 2y \quad \text{and} \quad f_y(x, y) = -2x + 3y^2.$$

Our critical numbers occur when our first order partial derivates are zero, so let

$$2x - 2y = 0 \quad \text{and} \quad -2x + 3y^2 = 0.$$

The first equation implies that all relative extrema must lie on $x = y$, so we're ready to choose (A), but let's keep going.

We need the critical numbers. Since $y = x$ and $-2x + 3y^2 = 0$,

$$-2x + 3x^2 = x(-2 + 3x) = 0 \quad \text{implies} \quad x = 0 \text{ or } x = 2/3.$$

It follows that our critical numbers are $(0, 0)$ and $(2/3, 2/3)$.

Next, we find $H_f(x, y)$. The second order partial derivatives are:

$$f_{xx}(x, y) = 2, \quad f_{xy}(x, y) = f_{yx}(x, y) = -2, \quad \text{and} \quad f_{yy}(x, y) = 6y.$$

Hence, $H_f(x, y) = 12y - 4$.

With the second derivatives test in mind, we examine our critical points.

$(0, 0)$: $H_f(0, 0) = -4 < 0$, so there is a saddle point at $(0, 0)$.

$(2/3, 2/3)$: $f_{xx}(2/3, 2/3) = 2 > 0$ and $H_f(2/3, 2/3) = 8 - 4 = 4 > 0$, so there is a relative minimum at $(2/3, 2/3)$.

Obviously, these results exclude (C), but could $(2/3, 2/3)$ be an absolute minimum? No. Why? Because f has no lower bound: fix x and you can see $f(x, y) = x^2 - 2xy + y^3 \to -\infty$ as $y \to -\infty$. ∎

Question 2.27. ───────────────────────────
We will use simultaneous equations to solve this problem. Let's eliminate the y variable.

$$2x + y - 3z = 0 \quad \text{implies} \quad -6x - 3y + 9z = 0.$$

So,

$$
\begin{array}{rrrrrrl}
  & -6x & - & 3y & + & 9z & = & 0 \\
+ & x & + & 3y & - & 2z & = & 7 \\
\hline
  & -5x &   &   & + & 7z & = & 7,
\end{array}
$$

or $z = 1 + 5x/7$. To remove the fraction, let $x = 7t$. This implies $z = 1 + 5t$. We were given that $2x + y - 3z = 0$, so

$$
\begin{aligned}
y &= -2x + 3z \\
  &= -2(7t) + 3(1 + 5t) \\
  &= 3 + t.
\end{aligned}
$$

Thus, the solution is $\{(x, y, x) : x = 7t, y = 3 + t, z = 1 + 5t, t \in \mathbb{R}\}$. We conclude that (D) is correct. ∎

Question 2.28. ───────────────────────────
Denote deletion of a side by a slash mark. The graph below satisfies the necessary criteria.

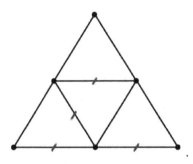

The correct answer must be (D). ∎

Question 2.29. ────────────────────────────

Let's find a counterexample to $e^f \sim e^g$. Consider $f(x) = x$ and $g(x) = x + 1$. It's clear $\lim_{x \to \infty} f(x)/g(x) = 1$. But

$$\lim_{x \to \infty} \frac{e^x}{e^{x+1}} = \lim_{x \to \infty} \frac{1}{e} = \frac{1}{e} \neq 1.$$

This is enough to conclude that (C) is correct and move on, but we're not being timed so let's verify that the others work.

First, $f^2 \sim g^2$.

$$\lim_{x \to \infty} \frac{\left(f(x)\right)^2}{\left(g(x)\right)^2} = \left(\lim_{x \to \infty} \frac{f(x)}{g(x)}\right)^2 = 1^2 = 1.$$

Next, $\sqrt{f} \sim \sqrt{g}$. The argument is very similar.

$$\lim_{x \to \infty} \frac{\sqrt{f(x)}}{\sqrt{g(x)}} = \sqrt{\lim_{x \to \infty} \frac{f(x)}{g(x)}} = \sqrt{1} = 1.$$

We continue by considering $f + g \sim 2g$.

$$\lim_{x \to \infty} \frac{f(x) + g(x)}{2g(x)} = \frac{1}{2} \lim_{x \to \infty} \frac{f(x)}{g(x)} + 1 = \frac{1}{2}(1 + 1) = 1.$$

Lastly, $g \sim f$.

$$\lim_{x \to \infty} \frac{g(x)}{f(x)} = \lim_{x \to \infty} \frac{1}{\dfrac{f(x)}{g(x)}} = \frac{1}{\displaystyle\lim_{x \to \infty} \frac{f(x)}{g(x)}} = \frac{1}{1} = 1.$$

∎

Question 2.30. ────────────────────────────

The negation of f *is one-to-one and onto Y* is f *is not one-to-one or f is not onto Y* (remember that *or* is inclusive). Statement R is f *is not one-to-one* and Q means f *is onto*, so not Q must mean f *is not onto*. We can conclude that R *or not Q* is the correct answer, and fill in the bubble for option (C). ■

Question 2.31.
It's easy to see that

$$\frac{dy}{dx} \longrightarrow \infty \quad \text{as} \quad |y| \longrightarrow \infty,$$

which narrows our selection down to (A) and (B). Since $dy/dx \geq 1$, we exclude choice (B) because the derivative of that function is about 0 when its graph intersects the y-axis. ■

Question 2.32.
We exclude property I because it is not necessarily true. The binary operation $\odot$ need not be commutative, and we would need to rearrange the factors of $(x \odot y)^n$ to obtain $x^n \odot y^n$.

Property II follows, because $\oplus$ is associative and commutative due to (2) and (3), respectively. The argument goes as follows:

$$n(x \oplus y) = \underbrace{(x \oplus y) \oplus (x \oplus y) \oplus \cdots \oplus (x \oplus y)}_{n \text{ times}}$$

$$= x \oplus (y \oplus x) \oplus y \oplus (x \oplus y) \oplus \ldots \oplus (x \oplus y)$$

$$= x \oplus (x \oplus y) \oplus y \oplus (x \oplus y) \oplus \ldots \oplus (x \oplus y)$$

$$= 2x \oplus 2y \oplus \underbrace{(x \oplus y) \oplus \ldots \oplus (x \oplus y)}_{n-2 \text{ times}}$$

$$= 2x \oplus (2y \oplus x) \oplus y \oplus (x \oplus y) \oplus \ldots \oplus (x \oplus y)$$

$$= 2x \oplus x \oplus 2y \oplus y \oplus (x \oplus y) \oplus \ldots \oplus (x \oplus y)$$

$$= 2x \oplus x \oplus (2y \oplus y) \oplus (x \oplus y) \oplus \ldots \oplus (x \oplus y)$$

$$= 3x \oplus 3y \oplus \underbrace{(x \oplus y) \oplus \ldots \oplus (x \oplus y)}_{n-3 \text{ times}}$$

$$\vdots$$

$$= nx \oplus ny.$$

Property III follows due to associativity which is guaranteed by (2). The argument is similar:

$$x^n \odot x^m = x^n \odot \underbrace{(x \odot x \odot \cdots \odot x)}_{m \text{ times}}$$

$$= x^n \odot \big(x \odot (x \odot \cdots \odot x)\big)$$

$$= (x^n \odot x) \odot (x \odot \cdots \odot x)$$

$$= x^{n+1} \odot \underbrace{(x \odot \cdots \odot x)}_{m-1 \text{ times}}$$

$$\vdots$$

$$= x^{n+m-1} \odot x$$

$$= x^{n+m}.$$

Thus, (D) is the best candidate. Note we assumed that computations for both $\oplus$ and $\odot$ are done from left to right when there were no parentheses. ∎

Question 2.33.

Let's go through the process. We plug in a = 273 and b = 110, and our first r = 273 mod 110 = 53. For the next step, a = 110 and b = 53, so r = 110 mod 53 = 4. Then a = 53, b = 4, so r = 53 mod 4 = 1. Then a = 4, b = 1, so r = 4 mod 1 = 0. Thus, our sequence of r's is 53, 4, 1, 0. This corresponds to the sequence in option (D), so we select it. ∎

Question 2.34.

Since the line containing the points on the spheres of minimum distance from each other also contains the centers of the spheres, all we need to do is calculate the distance between the centers of the spheres, and subtract the two radii. The centers of the two spheres are $(-3, 2, 4)$ and $(2, 1, 3)$, which implies that the distance between them is

$$d = \sqrt{(-3-2)^2 + (2-1)^2 + (4-3)^2} = \sqrt{25+1+1} = 3\sqrt{3}.$$

The radii of the two spheres are 1 and 2. It follows that the distance, between the points closest to each other, on the spheres is

$$3\sqrt{3} - 1 - 2 = 3(\sqrt{3} - 1).$$

The answer must be (E). ∎

Question 2.35.
First, the total number of permutations of men and women is 15!. To find the number of permutations where all the men are seated next to each other, consider the collection of men to be one unit, which gives us 10! permutations of the women and the "men-unit". Within the "men-unit", there are 6! ways to seat the group of men. It follows that there are a total of 6!10! ways to seat the group if all the men sit together. Thus, the probability that all the men will sit together is 6!10!/15!. Select (E)! ∎

Question 2.36.
All but (A) are claims equivalent to saying the columns of M are linearly independent.

Suppose M has linearly independent columns. This is equivalent to (B) which says that the only solution of $M\boldsymbol{x} = \boldsymbol{0}$ is $\boldsymbol{x} = \boldsymbol{0}$. Saying there is only one solution to the homogeneous equation is the same as saying (C) which claims $M\boldsymbol{x} = \boldsymbol{b}$ has only one solution for each $\boldsymbol{b}$. This is equivalent to saying M is invertible, which is (E). The matrix M is invertible if and only if its determinate is nonzero, claim (D).

To see why (A) isn't equivalent to the rest, consider

$$M = \begin{pmatrix} 1 & 0 & 0 & 0 & 1 \\ 0 & 1 & 0 & 0 & 1 \\ 0 & 0 & 1 & 0 & 1 \\ 0 & 0 & 0 & 1 & 1 \\ 0 & 0 & 0 & 0 & 0 \end{pmatrix}.$$

Clearly, the columns aren't linearly independent, though they are pairwise independent. ∎

Question 2.37. ─────────────────────────────

Let $z = x + iy$, where x and y are real numbers. Then $z^2 = (x + iy)^2 = x^2 - y^2 + 2ixy$ and $|z|^2 = x^2 + y^2$. So,

$$z^2 = |z|^2 \quad \text{implies} \quad ixy = y^2.$$

It follows that $y = 0$, because a real number can't equal an imaginary one. Thus, the equation must describe a line, which means (D) is correct. ∎

Question 2.38. ─────────────────────────────

The definition of the set $f^{-1}(Y)$ is $\{x \in A : f(x) \in Y\}$, where $Y \subseteq B$. As a result, $C \subseteq f^{-1}(f(C))$ because x in C implies $f(x)$ in $f(C)$ so x in $f^{-1}(f(C))$. Hence, the answer is (A). ∎

Question 2.39. ─────────────────────────────

In this situation, the *Law of cosines* tells us

$$s^2 = 1 + r^2 - 2r \cos 110° \quad \text{implies} \quad s = \sqrt{1 + r^2 - 2r \cos 110°}.$$

It follows that

$$\lim_{\substack{s \to \infty \\ r \to \infty}} (s - r) = \lim_{r \to \infty} \sqrt{1 + r^2 - 2r \cos 110°} - r$$

$$= \lim_{r \to \infty} \frac{1 + r^2 - 2r \cos 110° - r^2}{\sqrt{1 + r^2 - 2r \cos 110°} + r}$$

$$= \lim_{r \to \infty} \frac{1 - 2r \cos 110°}{\sqrt{1 + r^2 - 2r \cos 110°} + r}$$

$$= \lim_{r \to \infty} \frac{\frac{1}{r} - 2 \cos 110°}{\sqrt{\frac{1}{r^2} + 1 - \frac{2 \cos 110°}{r}} + 1}$$

$$= - \cos 110°$$

$$= \cos 70°.$$

Because cosine is positive and decreases monotonically on the interval $[0, 90°]$, we have $0 < \cos 70° < \cos 60° = 1/2 < 1$. We conclude that the solution must be (B). ∎

Question 2.40. ————————————————————————

Consider

$$f(x) := \begin{cases} 0, & \text{if } x \geq 1/2 \\ x - 1/2, & \text{if } x < 1/2 \end{cases} \quad \text{and} \quad g(x) := \begin{cases} x - 1/2, & \text{if } x \geq 1/2 \\ 0, & \text{if } x < 1/2. \end{cases}$$

Both of these functions are continuous and real-valued on the closed interval $[0, 1]$, and $(fg)(x) = 0$. Pick (C)! ∎

Question 2.41. ————————————————————————

Green's theorem states:

> Let C be a piecewise smooth, simple closed curve in the xy-plane, which is oriented counterclockwise. Suppose D is the region bounded by C. Assume L and M are functions of x and y and have continuous partial derivatives on an open region containing D. Then
>
> $$\oint_C L \, dx + M \, dy = \iint_D \frac{\partial M}{\partial x} - \frac{\partial L}{\partial y} \, dA.$$

In our case,

$$\oint_C (2x - y) \, dx + (x + 3y) \, dy$$

$$= \iint_{\{(x,y):\ x^2+y^2<1\}} \frac{\partial}{\partial x}(x + 3y) - \frac{\partial}{\partial y}(2x - y) \, dA$$

$$= \iint_{\{(x,y):\ x^2+y^2<1\}} 2 \, dA$$

$$= 2\pi.$$

We shade in (E) and continue. Note $\iint_{\{(x,y):\ x^2+y^2<1\}} dA$ is simply the area of a circle of radius 1, so we know $\iint_{\{(x,y):\ x^2+y^2<1\}} dA = \pi$ before we perform any computations. ∎

Question 2.42. —————————————————————————
This is simply an application of a few *probability properties*. Consider the following argument:

$$P(X > 3 \text{ or } Y > 3) = 1 - P(X \leq 3 \text{ and } Y \leq 3)$$
$$= 1 - P(X \leq 3) \cdot P(X \leq 3)$$
$$= 1 - \left(P(X \leq 3)\right)^2$$
$$= 1 - \left(\frac{1}{2} + \frac{1}{4} + \frac{1}{8}\right)^2$$
$$= 1 - \frac{49}{64}$$
$$= \frac{15}{64}.$$

Mark option (B)! ∎

Question 2.43. —————————————————————————
Euler's formula says that for all θ in $\mathbb{C}$,

$$e^{i\theta} = \cos\theta + i\sin\theta.$$

So,

$$z = e^{2\pi i/5} \quad \text{implies} \quad z^5 = e^{2\pi i} = \cos 2\pi + i\sin 2\pi = 1.$$

It follows that

$$z^5 - 1 = (z - 1)(z^4 + z^3 + z^2 + z + 1) = 0.$$

Since $z \neq 1$,

$$z^4 + z^3 + z^2 + z + 1 = 0.$$

From here, simplification is done by means of substitution and factorization:

$$1 + z^2 + z^3 + 5z^4 + 4z^5 + 4z^6 + 4z^7 + 4z^8 + 5z^9$$
$$= (1 + z^2 + z^3 + z^4) + 4z^4(1 + z + z^2 + z^3 + z^4) + 5z^9$$
$$= 0 + 4z^4(0) + 5z^9$$
$$= 5z^9$$

Let's substitute $e^{2\pi i/5}$ into the equation for z:

$$5z^9 = 5\left(e^{2\pi i/5}\right)^9 = 5e^{18\pi i/5}.$$

Since $18\pi i/5 = 3\pi i + 3\pi i/5$ and $e^{3\pi i} = -1$, we see

$$5z^9 = 5e^{3\pi i}e^{3\pi i/5} = 5(-1)e^{3\pi i/5} = -5e^{3\pi/5}.$$

Hence, (E) is correct. ∎

Question 2.44.

The probability distribution for the number of heads occurring on a fair coin is a *binomial distribution*. In general, for a binomial distribution:

- The expected value is $\mu = np$ and
- the standard deviation is $\sigma = \sqrt{np(1-p)}$,

where n is the number of trials and p is the probability of success. It's also helpful to note that for large n, the normal distribution of mean μ and standard deviation σ is a good approximation of the binomial distribution of mean μ and standard deviation σ.

Onto our problem: We were given that $n = 100$ and $p = 1/2$, so

$$\mu = 100\left(\frac{1}{2}\right) = 50 \quad \text{and} \quad \sigma = \sqrt{100\left(\frac{1}{2}\right)\left(\frac{1}{2}\right)} = 5.$$

Since the probability of obtaining any specific number of heads or tails is quite low, we exclude (A). As mentioned above, the normal distribution of mean 50 and standard deviation 5 is a good approximation for the binomial distribution, so the probability $T \geq 60$ is low, because it's two standard deviations from the expected result of 50. As such, exclude (B). Exclude (E) because those results are even further away from the mean. We've narrowed it down to (C) and (D). Choice (D) is equivalent to stating $48 \leq H \leq 52$. Since more events in (D) are closer to the expected value of 50 than those in $51 \leq H \leq 55$, we conclude the solution is (D). ∎

Question 2.45. —————————————————————

This is a simple application of *pigeonhole principle*. However, we won't reference it directly in our argument.

Statement I is true. Since there will always be twenty-one points, less in one sector implies more in another. As such, to minimize the number of points in the sector with the most, we distribute the points as homogeneously as possible. So, we would want to put $21/5 = 4.2$ points in each sector, but this is impossible since we can't put 0.2 points in a sector. Thus, the most homogeneous distribution would have 5 points in one sector.

Statement II is a lie. The situation described in option I proves that II isn't necessarily true since we could have 4 points in four sectors and 5 in the remaining sector.

Statement III is a legitimate proposition. Consider new sectors created by combining the adjacent sectors in the picture above. Each sector is adjacent to two others, so we double counted the old sectors. Therefore, we've also double counted the number of points, so our new sectors have a combined total of 42 points. There is a total of 5 new sectors. To minimize the number of points in the new sector with the most, we want to distribute the points as homogeneously as possible. That means we want to put $42/5 = 8.4$ points in each new sector. But there cannot be a fraction of a point in a sector so we would put 8 in all but one and 9 in the last sector.

We conclude that (D) is correct because only I and III are true. ∎

Question 2.46. —————————————————————

We need the following identity:

Let z be a complex number, and $|z|$ be the modulus of z. Then $z = |z|e^{i\theta} = |z|(\cos\theta + i\sin\theta)$, for some θ.

Since the modulus of each element in G is 1, the identity simplifies to the claim that for each z in G there is a θ such that $z = e^{i\theta}$. Onto our problem.

First, we note that exponentiation is a homomorphism. To prove this, consider any integer k and the map $z \mapsto z^k$. Then for z_1 and

z_2 in G, we have
$$z_1 z_2 \mapsto (z_1 z_2)^k = z_1^k z_2^k,$$
due to rules of exponentiation. Hence, this is a homomorphism. From here, choice II follows immediately. Choice I also follows, because $z \mapsto \bar{z}$ is the same as $z \mapsto z^{-1}$ since
$$z^{-1} = e^{-i\theta} = \cos(-\theta) + i\sin(-\theta) = \cos\theta - i\sin\theta.$$

All we need to do is prove III. Since a homomorphism is completely determined by where it sends its group's generators and i generates G, all that's left to show is that every map takes i to i^k for some integer k. Due to the fact that $i = e^{i\pi/2}$, it's not too tough to see that
$$i \mapsto 1 = i^4, \quad i \mapsto -1 = i^2, \quad i \mapsto -i = i^3, \quad \text{and} \quad i \mapsto i = i^1.$$

Fill in the bubble for (E)! ∎

Question 2.47. ───────────────────────────
Let $C := \{\gamma(t) : a \le t \le b\}$, where $\gamma : \mathbb{R} \to \mathbb{R}^3$ is differentiable in each coordinate. Then the *work* done by a vector field $\boldsymbol{F}$ over the path C is
$$W = \int_C \boldsymbol{F} \cdot d\gamma = \int_a^b \boldsymbol{F} \cdot \gamma'(t)\, dt.$$
In our case, the formula implies
$$W = \int_{\{(t,t^2,t^3):\, 0 \le t \le 1\}} (-1,0,1) \cdot d\gamma = \int_0^1 (-1,0,1) \cdot (1,2t,3t^2)\, dt.$$

All that is left is to take the dot product and use first semester Calculus techniques to evaluate:
$$W = \int_0^1 -1 + 3t^2\, dt = -t + t^3 \Big|_0^1 = -1 + 1 - (0) = 0.$$

This result implies (C) is correct. ∎

Question 2.48. ————————————————————
Inane ramblings: The argument is valid, so select (A). There's a moral to this question: Don't assume that it can't be any particular answer until you've examined the math. According to the GRE booklet, 63% of test-takers got this question wrong. I assume because they thought (A) was the "sucker's answer" and worked themselves to death trying to find nonexistent errors. ∎

Question 2.49. ————————————————————
We will use the finite case of the *Fundamental theorem of finitely generated abelian groups.*

> Let G be a finite abelian group of order m. Then it is isomorphic to an expression of the form
>
> $$\mathbb{Z}_{k_1} \times \mathbb{Z}_{k_2} \times \ldots \times \mathbb{Z}_{k_n},$$
>
> where k_i divides both k_{i+1} and m for all $i = 1, 2, \ldots, n-1$ and $m = k_1 \cdot k_2 \cdot \ldots \cdot k_n$.

In our situation, we can't have a k_i greater than 4 because that would imply that the characteristic of G would be greater than 4. Thus, the only groups with the property that $x + x + x + x = 0$ are

$$\mathbb{Z}_4 \times \mathbb{Z}_4, \quad \mathbb{Z}_2 \times \mathbb{Z}_2 \times \mathbb{Z}_4, \quad \text{and} \quad \mathbb{Z}_2 \times \mathbb{Z}_2 \times \mathbb{Z}_2 \times \mathbb{Z}_2.$$

It must be (D). ∎

Question 2.50. ————————————————————
Statement I is a lie. For example,

$$A := \begin{pmatrix} 0 & -1 \\ 1 & 0 \end{pmatrix} \quad \text{implies} \quad A^2 = \begin{pmatrix} -1 & 0 \\ 0 & -1 \end{pmatrix}.$$

Statement II is true, because $\det(A^2) = (\det(A))^2 \geq 0$.

Statement III is false. What if the eigenvalues of A are $\lambda_1 = 1$ and $\lambda_2 = -1$? Doesn't that imply the only eigenvalue of A^2 would be 1?

As a result, (B) is correct. ∎

Question 2.51. ────────────────────────────────

It's not too tough to see

$$\int_0^\infty \lfloor x \rfloor e^{-x} dx = \sum_{n=1}^\infty \int_n^{n+1} n e^{-x} dx.$$

The next few steps are just simple math

$$\sum_{n=1}^\infty \int_n^{n+1} n e^{-x} dx = \sum_{n=1}^\infty -n e^{-n-1} + n e^{-n}$$

$$= \sum_{n=1}^\infty \frac{n(e-1)}{e^{n+1}}$$

$$= (1 - e^{-1}) \sum_{n=1}^\infty \frac{n}{e^n}$$

$$= (1 - e^{-1}) \sum_{n=1}^\infty n \left(e^{-1}\right)^n.$$

We need to find a formula for

$$\sum_{n=1}^\infty n x^n.$$

First, recall the formula for an infinite geometric series

$$\frac{1}{1-x} = \sum_{n=0}^\infty x^n,$$

when $|x| < 1$. It follows that

$$\frac{d}{dx} \left(\frac{1}{1-x} \right) = \frac{1}{(1-x)^2} = \frac{d}{dx} \left(\sum_{n=0}^\infty x^n \right) = \sum_{n=1}^\infty n x^{n-1}.$$

Multiplying both sides by x yields

$$\frac{x}{(1-x)^2} = \sum_{n=1}^\infty n x^n.$$

81

Notice that the left side of the equation above is what we're looking for, where $x = e^{-1}$. Thus,

$$(1 - e^{-1}) \sum_{n=1}^{\infty} n \left(e^{-1}\right)^n = (1 - e^{-1}) \frac{e^{-1}}{(1 - e^{-1})^2} = \frac{1}{e - 1},$$

which means (B) is correct. ∎

Question 2.52. ————————————————————
Option (B) is true. Here's why: Recall that $\mathbb{Q}$ is *dense* in $\mathbb{R}$, i.e. $\text{cl}(\mathbb{Q}) = \mathbb{R}$ where cl denotes the closure of a set. It follows that if A is closed $\text{cl}(\mathbb{Q}) = \mathbb{R} \subseteq \text{cl}(A) = A \subseteq \text{cl}(\mathbb{R}) = \mathbb{R}$. Thus, $A = \mathbb{R}$.

Let's see why the others are false. To see why (A) isn't true, consider $A = \mathbb{R} \setminus \{\pi\}$; the set A is open because for each x in A, the open ball centered at x with radius $|x - \pi|/2$ is contained in A. To disprove (C), consider $A := \mathbb{Q} \cup (0, 1)$. The same counterexample disproves (D). Choice (E) is disproved by $A = \mathbb{Q}$, because $\sqrt{2}$ is a limit point of $\mathbb{Q}$ not contained within $\mathbb{Q}$. ∎

Question 2.53. ————————————————————
The minimum value of $f(x, y, z) := x + 4z$ occurs on the boundary of the solid sphere $x^2 + y^2 + z^2 \leq 2$, i.e. the minimum value for f occurs when $x^2 + y^2 + z^2 = 2$.

We need the *method of Lagrange multipliers*:

> Suppose $f(x, y, x)$ had first order partial derivatives, and the values x, y, and z satisfy the constraint $g(x, y, z) = k$, where k is a constant. Then relative extrema occur at the points (x, y, z) that satisfy
>
> $$f_x(x, y, x) = \lambda g_x(x, y, z), \quad f_y(x, y, z) \qquad = \lambda g_y(x, y, z),$$
> $$\text{and} \quad f_z(x, y, z) = \lambda g_z(x, y, z)$$
>
> for some λ in $\mathbb{R}$.

Obviously, the function we wish to maximize is $f(x, y, z) = x + 4z$ and our constraint is $g(x, y, z) := x^2 + y^2 + z^2 = 2$. The method of

82

Lagrange multipliers tells us

$$1 = 2\lambda x, \quad 0 = 2\lambda y, \quad \text{and} \quad 4 = 2\lambda z.$$

A bit of algebra shows $y = 0$, and $z = 4x$. Substituting the right sides into the appropriate coordinates of g yields

$$\begin{aligned} g(x, 0, 4x) &= x^2 + (4x)^2 \\ &= x^2 + 16x^2 \\ &= 17x^2 \\ &= 2. \end{aligned}$$

It follows that

$$x = \pm\sqrt{\frac{2}{17}} = \pm\frac{\sqrt{34}}{17} \quad \text{and} \quad z = \pm\frac{4\sqrt{34}}{17},$$

which means our relative extrema are

$$f\left(\pm\frac{\sqrt{34}}{17}, 0, \pm\frac{4\sqrt{34}}{17}\right) = \pm\sqrt{34}.$$

Since there are no endpoints to test and we are on a compact domain, relative extrema are absolute extrema. Thus, the minimum value of f satisfying $x^2 + y^2 + z^2 = 2$ is $-\sqrt{34}$, and we pick (C). ∎

Question 2.54. —————————————————————

We can form a $45°$–$45°$–$90°$ special right triangle whose hypotenuse has the center of the large circle and a small circle as endpoints. If the small circles have radius r, then each leg of the right triangle we formed also has length r. This implies that the right triangle's hypotenuse has length $r\sqrt{2}$.

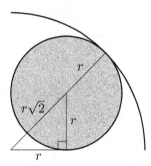

Let's find the ratio of the shaded area in figure 1 to the area of the big circle in figure 1. Suppose the big circle has radius R. The picture above shows that

$$r + r\sqrt{2} = r(1 + \sqrt{2}) = R.$$

It follows that $r = R/(1+\sqrt{2})$. Hence, the ratio of the four shaded circles in figure 1 to the area of the big circle is

$$\frac{4\pi \left(\frac{R}{1+\sqrt{2}}\right)^2}{\pi R^2} = \left(\frac{2}{1 + \sqrt{2}}\right)^2.$$

Since the ratio of the areas of the big and small circles in figure 1 is the same as the ratio of the areas of the shaded circles in figure 2 and figure 1, we conclude the answer is

$$\left(\frac{2}{1 + \sqrt{2}}\right)^2$$

and we fill in (E). ∎

Question 2.55. ─────────────────────────────────

Zeros are added in the ordinary decimal representation of $k!$ every time another factor of 10 appears. Since there are more even numbers than multiples of 5, at least one new factor of 10 appears in $k!$ every time k is a multiple of 5.

Let's obtain some rules to help us complete this problem. The number 5! ends in one zero, 10! ends in two zeros, and 15! ends in three. The pattern continues until we reach 25!, which ends in six zeros since 25 has two factors of 5. It's clear this generalizes to the following rule: When k has two factors of 5, two zeros are added to the decimal representation of $k!$. Going from 124! to 125! adds three new zeros since 125 has three factors of 5. It's clear this generalizes to the following: When k has three factors of 5, three zeros are added to the decimal representation of $k!$. In general: When k has n factors of 5, n new zeros appear in the decimal representation of $k!$.

From here, we consider values of k and use the principles outlined above. Suppose $k = 400$. Then $400! = 400 \cdot 399 \cdots \ldots \cdot 1$ has 80 factors which are divisible by 5, 16 are divisible by 25, and 3 are divisible by 125. It follows that 400! has $80 + 16 + 3 = 99$ zeros when written in its ordinary decimal representation. Clearly 401!, 402!, 403!, and 404! will also have 99 zeros since 5 does not divide 401, 402, 403, or 404. This is enough to select (D). ∎

Question 2.56. ─────────────────────────────────

For those unfamiliar with the definition of a *metric*, see the glossary at the end of this booklet.

The function ω fails the triangle inequality, so it cannot be a metric. For example, say $x = 1, y = 0$, and $z = 1/2$; then $\omega(1,0) = 1$ and $\omega(1,1/2) + \omega(1/2,0) = 1/4 + 1/4 = 1/2$.

This is where we would choose (E) and move on during the test, but let's make a few more remarks. Verifying that (A)–(C) are metrics doesn't add much insight. Instead, we'll explain why we would want to examine τ and ω first during the GRE:

(A) It looks like δ behaves like the discrete metric.

(B) It looks like ρ behaves like the Euclidian metric for values "close" together, and behaves like the discrete metric elsewhere.

(C) It looks like σ is equivalent to the Euclidian metric.

Now let's verify that τ is a metric. We know $d(x, y) = |x - y|$ is a metric, and non-negativity and symmetry of τ follow directly from this. Next, to prove τ passes the triangle inequality criterion, note that

$$f(x) := \frac{x}{1 + x}$$

is monotonically increasing for all non-negative numbers. You can prove this, for example, by taking the derivative. Therefore, for all x, y, and z,

$$\begin{aligned}
\tau(x, y) &= f\left(|x - y|\right) \\
&\leq f\left(|x - z| + |z - y|\right) \\
&= \frac{|x - z| + |z - y|}{1 + |x - z| + |z - y|} \\
&= \frac{|x - z|}{1 + |x - z| + |z - y|} + \frac{|z - y|}{1 + |x - z| + |z - y|} \\
&\leq \frac{|x - z|}{1 + |x - z|} + \frac{|z - y|}{1 + |z - y|} \\
&= \tau(x, z) + \tau(z, y).
\end{aligned}$$

∎

Question 2.57. ────────────────────────────

Since n^n grows far more rapidly than $n!$ and

$$0 \leq \frac{x^{2n}}{1 + x^{2n}} < 1$$

for all x, the answer is (E). However, let's go through this more thoroughly for those less familiar with series.

We have

$$0 \leq \frac{x^{2n}}{1 + x^{2n}} < 1 \quad \text{implies} \quad 0 \leq \frac{n! x^{2n}}{n^n \left(1 + x^{2n}\right)} \leq \frac{n!}{n^n},$$

86

for $n = 1, 2, 3, \ldots$. So convergence of $\sum \frac{n!}{n^n}$ implies convergence of $\sum \frac{n! x^{2n}}{n^n (1+x^{2n})}$.

We will use the *ratio test* to prove $\sum \frac{n!}{n^n}$ converges:

$$\lim_{n \to \infty} \left| \frac{\frac{(n+1)!}{(n+1)^{n+1}}}{\frac{n!}{n^n}} \right| = \lim_{n \to \infty} \frac{(n+1)!}{(n+1)^{n+1}} \frac{n^n}{n!}$$

$$= \lim_{n \to \infty} \frac{(n+1)}{(n+1)^{n+1}} \frac{n^n}{1}$$

$$= \lim_{n \to \infty} \left(\frac{n}{n+1} \right)^n$$

$$= \frac{1}{e}$$

$$< 1$$

Before we move on to the next problem, let's see why

$$\lim_{t \to \infty} \left(\frac{t}{t+1} \right)^t = \frac{1}{e}.$$

Let

$$y := \left(\frac{t}{t+1} \right)^t.$$

Then, taking the natural log of both sides and using the power rule for logarithms on the right side of the equation yields,

$$\log y = t \log \frac{t}{t+1}.$$

It follows that

$$\lim_{t \to \infty} \log y = \lim_{t \to \infty} t \log \frac{t}{t+1} = \lim_{t \to \infty} \frac{\log \left(\frac{t}{t+1} \right)}{\frac{1}{t}}.$$

We have a 0/0 scenario since $\log \left(\frac{t}{t+1} \right) \to 0$ as $t \to \infty$, so we can use *L'Hôspital's rule* which we denote by "LH":

$$\lim_{t\to\infty} \log y \overset{LH}{=} \lim_{t\to\infty} \frac{\frac{t+1}{t} \cdot \frac{1}{(t+1)^2}}{-\frac{1}{t^2}}$$

$$= \lim_{t\to\infty} -\frac{t}{t+1}$$

$$= \lim_{t\to\infty} \frac{-1}{1+\frac{1}{t}}$$

$$= -1.$$

Furthermore,

$$\lim_{t\to\infty} \log y = -1 \quad \text{implies} \quad \lim_{t\to\infty} y = \frac{1}{e}.$$

A list of *logarithm properties* is located in the glossary. ■

Question 2.58. ────────────────────────────────

Let's introduce some notation. Since A and B are similar, let's say $PAP^{-1} = B$. Also, let $\text{tr}(C)$ denote the trace of C.

Onto our problem: Property I is true. Suppose $PAP^{-1} = B$. Then

$$P(A - 2I)P^{-1} = PAP^{-1} - 2PIP^{-1}$$

$$= PAP^{-1} - 2I$$

$$= B - 2I.$$

Property II is valid. Recall $\text{tr}(AB) = \text{tr}(BA)$. In our case,

$$\text{tr}(B) = \text{tr}\Big(P(AP^{-1})\Big) = \text{tr}\Big((AP^{-1})P\Big) = \text{tr}(AI) = \text{tr}(A).$$

Property III holds too. If $PAP^{-1} = B$, then

$$B^{-1} = (PAP^{-1})^{-1} = (P^{-1})^{-1}(PA)^{-1} = PA^{-1}P^{-1}.$$

Shade the bubble for (E). ■

Question 2.59. ————————————————————————————

Recall the *necessary and sufficient condition* for a function to be *analytic*:

> Let $z = x + iy$. The function $f(z) = u(x, y) + iv(x, y)$ is analytic at z if and only if $u_x(x, y) = v_y(x, y)$ and $u_y(x, y) = -v_x(x, y)$.

Hence, if f is analytic, then

$$g_y(x, y) = \frac{\partial}{\partial x}(2x + 3y) \quad \text{and} \quad g_x(x, y) = -\frac{\partial}{\partial y}(2x + 3y)$$
$$= 2 \qquad\qquad\qquad\qquad\qquad = -3.$$

It follows that

$$g(x, y) = 2y + h_1(x) \quad \text{and} \quad g(x, y) = -3x + h_2(y),$$

where h_1 and h_2 are functions of x and y, respectively, or a constant function. In conjunction, for some constant C, these two expressions imply

$$g(x, y) = -3x + 2y + C.$$

Since $g(2, 3) = 1$ and

$$g(2, 3) = -3(2) + 2(3) + C = C,$$

we have $C = 1$. Thus,

$$g(7, 3) = -3(7) + 2(3) + 1$$
$$= -15 + 1$$
$$= -14.$$

Ergo, (A) is right. ∎

Question 2.60. ————————————————————————————

The Dihedral group of order 10 is, by definition, the group of symmetries of a pentagon. There's no reason to believe the symmetries of a pentagram are any different. We select (E). ∎

Question 2.61. ——————————————————————

A list of definitions for *cardinal arithmetic* is contained in the glossary. Also, recall the *Schröder-Berstein theorem*, which states:

> For sets A and B, $|A| \leq |B|$ and $|B| \leq |A|$ implies $|A| = |B|$.

Onto our problem:

(A) Recall $|\mathbb{R}| = 2^{\aleph_0}$.

(B) $\left| \{f \mid f : \mathbb{Z} \to \mathbb{Z}\} \right| = \aleph_0^{\aleph_0}$, and

$$2^{\aleph_0} \leq \aleph_0^{\aleph_0} \leq \left(2^{\aleph_0}\right)^{\aleph_0} = 2^{\aleph_0 \cdot \aleph_0} = 2^{\aleph_0}.$$

Thus, by the Schröder-Berstein theorem, we conclude

$$\left| \{f \mid f : \mathbb{Z} \to \mathbb{Z}\} \right| = 2^{\aleph_0}.$$

(C) It's clear $\left| \{f \mid f : \mathbb{R} \to \{0,1\}\} \right| = 2^{2^{\aleph_0}}$.

(D) Let $\mathcal{F}$ denote the set of finite subsets of $\mathbb{R}$. Because $f : \mathbb{R} \to \mathcal{F}$ defined by $f : x \mapsto \{x\}$ is one-to-one, it's clear $2^{\aleph_0} \leq |\mathcal{F}|$. Let $\mathcal{F}_n$ denote the set of subsets of $\mathbb{R}$ with n elements. Then

$$|\mathcal{F}| = \sum_{n=0}^{\infty} |\mathcal{F}_n|$$
$$\leq \sum_{n=1}^{\infty} 2^{\aleph_0}$$
$$= \aleph_0 \cdot 2^{\aleph_0}$$
$$= 2^{\aleph_0}.$$

So, by the Schröder-Berstein theorem, $|\mathcal{F}| = 2^{\aleph_0}$.

(E) It's clear the set of polynomials has the same cardinality as $\mathcal{F}$.

Since $2^{2^{\aleph_0}}$ is different than the others, the correct answer must be (C). ∎

Question 2.62. ───────────────────────────────

Property I must be true. The argument goes as follows. The continuous image of a compact space is compact. Thus, for f continuous and real-valued, $f(K) \subseteq \mathbb{R}$ must be compact. By the *Heine-Borel theorem*, $f(K)$ must be closed and bounded.

Property II is also true. We'll prove it using the other direction of the Heine–Borel theorem. If K were unbounded, then the real-valued function $f(x) := \|x\|$, where $\| \cdot \|$ denotes the Euclidian metric, would be unbounded. If K weren't closed, then it wouldn't contain one of its limit points, say ℓ. Then $f(x) := 1/\|x - \ell\|$ would be an unbounded continuous function. Thus, since K is a closed and bounded subset of $\mathbb{R}^n$, it must be compact.

Property III isn't valid. Consider $[0,1] \cup [2,3]$; clearly that's a compact set and it's not connected.

Pick (D), and carry on. ∎

Question 2.63. ───────────────────────────────

The graph of f has a horizontal tangent line when $f'(x) = 0$. Obviously, this means we need to find the derivative. For $x \neq 0$, $f(x) = xe^{-x^2 - x^{-2}}$. Therefore,

$$f'(x) = e^{-x^2 - x^{-2}} + x(-2x + 2x^{-3})e^{-x^2 - x^{-2}}$$
$$= \left(1 - 2x^2 + 2x^{-2}\right)e^{-x^2 - x^{-2}}$$
$$= \frac{-2x^4 + x^2 + 2}{x^2}e^{-x^2 - x^{-2}}$$

for $x \neq 0$. It's easy to see $f'(x) = 0$ when $-2x^4 + x^2 + 2 = 0$ which implies

$$x^2 = \frac{-1 \pm \sqrt{17}}{-4} = \frac{1 \mp \sqrt{17}}{4}.$$

Since $x^2 \geq 0$ we exclude $(1 - \sqrt{17})/4$ as a possibility. So, we've found two values of x that do the job so far. Namely,

$$x = \pm \frac{\sqrt{1 + \sqrt{17}}}{2}.$$

The only other time, possibly, when $f'(x)$ could equal 0 is at $x = 0$. For this case, we need to go back to the derivative definition:

$$f'(0) = \lim_{h \to 0} \frac{f(h) - f(0)}{h}$$

$$= \lim_{h \to 0} \frac{he^{-h^2 - h^{-2}}}{h}$$

$$= \lim_{h \to 0} e^{-h^2 - h^{-2}}$$

$$= 0.$$

Note $-h^2 - h^{-2} \to -\infty$ as $h \to 0$. Thus, there are a total of three values of x that make f parallel to the x-axis, so (D) is correct. ∎

Question 2.64. ——————————————————————
First, note

$$f(x) = \lim_{n \to \infty} \frac{x^n}{1 + x^n} = \begin{cases} 1/2, & x = 1 \\ 0, & 0 \le x < 1. \end{cases}$$

As such, $\{f_n\}$ converges pointwise, so I is true. However, $\{f_n\}$ does not converge uniformly to f by the contrapositive of the *uniform convergence theorem*, which disproves II. Here's the uniform convergence theorem:

> Suppose $\{f_n\}$ is a sequence of continuous functions that converge pointwise to the function f. If $\{f_n\}$ converges uniformly to f on an interval S, then f is continuous on S.

Lastly, III is true. One way to make this conclusion is by considering the fact that the set of discontinuities of f has measure 0. To give a more intuitive argument for III, the area under the graph of $f_n(x)$ goes to zero as n goes to infinity, so $\int_0^1 f_n(x)\, dx \to 0$ as $n \to \infty$. Clearly, $\int_0^1 f(x)\, dx = 0$, since there's no area under a point.

Option (D) is our choice. ∎

Question 2.65. ——————————————

Statement I is true. Consider $f(x) := \big| \sin(2\pi x) \big|$; $f(1/4) = 1$, $f(1/2) = 0$, and every value between follows from the *Intermediate value theorem*.

Statement II is false. The image of a compact set under a continuous map is compact. It follows that $f([0,1])$ must be compact when f is continuous. But the *Heine-Borel theorem* implies $f([0,1])$ must be closed and $(0,1)$ is not closed. Thus, $f([0,1]) \neq (0,1)$, if f is continuous.

Statement III is also an untruth. Suppose for the sake of contradiction that $g : (0,1) \to [0,1]$ is one-to-one and onto. If g is one-to-one, then it must be monotonic. Since g is onto there exists an x_1 in $(0,1)$ such that $g(x_1) = 1$. But this means g must be increasing for values of x less than x_1 and decreasing for values greater than x_1. This contradicts monotonicity.

Ergo, the answer must be (B). ■

Question 2.66. ——————————————

Statement I is false. Consider the quaternions. Since every nonzero element has an inverse, there are no proper ideals. Furthermore, 1 is an element of the quaternion. So all the criteria listed in the question are satisfied. But $ij = k$ and $ji = -k$.

Statement II is true. Let x be an arbitrary element in $R \setminus \{0\}$. We will prove x has an inverse. Consider $xR := \{xr : r \in R\}$. We want to prove that xR is a right ideal. Let's first verify that xR is a subgroup.

> Closed under addition: Suppose xr and xs are in xR. Then $xr + xs = x(r + s)$ is in xR.

> Contains the additive identity: This is clear, since $x0 = 0$.

> Contains additive inverses: It's clear $x(-r)$ is in xR,

and

$$x(-r) + xr = xr + x(-r)$$
$$= x(r - r)$$
$$= x0$$
$$= 0.$$

We know xR is a right ideal, because $(xr)s = x(rs)$ is in xR for all s in R. It follow that $xR = R$. This is because $x = x1$ is in xR and the only right ideals are $\{0\}$ and R. Hence, there is x' in R such that $xx' = 1$, so every nonzero element must have a right inverse because $x \neq 0$ was arbitrary. The last step is to prove x' is also a left inverse. We have $(x'x)(x'x) = x'(xx')x = x'x$. By multiplying both sides of $(x'x)(x'x) = x'x$ by the right inverse of $x'x$, we conclude $x'x = 1$. Thus, every nonzero element has an inverse, which proves R is a division ring.

Statement III is false. Consider $\mathbb{Z}_3$. It's a ring, and $\mathbb{Z}_3$ only has trivial ideals, since it's a field.

Select (B)! ∎

Chapter 3

GR9768 Solutions

Question 3.1. ──────────────────────────

Using the *Fundamental theorem of Calculus*, it follows that $F'(x) = \log x$, since the lower limit is a constant. The answer is (C). ∎

Question 3.2. ──────────────────────────

Let's look at a few iterations:

$$F(2) = 2 + \frac{1}{2}, \quad F(3) = 2 + \frac{1}{2} + \frac{1}{2} \quad \text{and} \quad F(4) = 2 + \frac{1}{2}(2) + \frac{1}{2}$$
$$= 2 + \frac{1}{2}(2), \qquad\qquad = 2 + \frac{1}{2}(3).$$

From here, it's not too tough to see

$$F(n) = 2 + \frac{1}{2}(n - 1).$$

Therefore,

$$F(101) = 2 + \frac{1}{2}(101 - 1) = 52,$$

and we select (D). ∎

Question 3.3.

The standard practice for finding the inverse of a matrix M is to put the matrix $(M|I)$ into reduced row-echelon form, where I is the $n \times n$ identity matrix. After this has been completed the right side of the augmented matrix will be M^{-1}. However, there is a formula for the *inverse of a* 2×2 *invertible matrix*. If

$$A := \begin{pmatrix} a & b \\ c & d \end{pmatrix}, \quad \text{then} \quad A^{-1} = \frac{1}{ad - bc} \begin{pmatrix} d & -b \\ -c & a \end{pmatrix}.$$

This immediately gives us

$$\begin{pmatrix} a & -b \\ b & a \end{pmatrix}^{-1} = \frac{1}{a^2 + b^2} \begin{pmatrix} a & b \\ -b & a \end{pmatrix},$$

so (C) is correct. ∎

Question 3.4.

Let's find our bounds of integration. To find b, we will compute the two integrals:

$$\int_0^b x \, dx = \left. \frac{x^2}{2} \right|_0^b \quad \text{and} \quad \int_0^b x^2 \, dx = \left. \frac{x^3}{3} \right|_0^b$$
$$= \frac{b^2}{2} \qquad\qquad\qquad = \frac{b^3}{3}.$$

It follows that $b^2/2 = b^3/3$, which implies $b = 3/2$. To find the lower bound of integration, set $x^2 = x$. This implies $x = 0$ or $x = 1$. The latter x-value is the desired result. As such, we will integrate over the interval $[1, 3/2]$.

Since $y = x^2$ is above $y = x$ when $1 \le x \le 3/2$, the shaded region in the figure has area

$$\int_1^{3/2} x^2 - x \, dx = \left. \frac{x^3}{3} - \frac{x^2}{2} \right|_1^{3/2} = \frac{1}{6}.$$

Pick (B)! ∎

Question 3.5. —————————————————————————
Using the *first derivative test*, it's clear that f has a relative minimum at $x \approx -3$, a relative maximum at $x \approx 6$, and a relative minimum at $x \approx 10$. This is enough to conclude that the solution is (E). ■

Question 3.6. —————————————————————————
Let's take a look at the first few p's:

$$
\begin{aligned}
p &= 0 \quad \text{when} \quad i = 1 \\
p &= 1 \quad \text{when} \quad i = 2 \\
p &= 2 \quad \text{when} \quad i = 4
\end{aligned}
$$

$$\vdots$$

$$p = n \quad \text{when} \quad i = 2^n.$$

From here, we simply note the first $i = 2^n$ that is greater than 999 occurs when $n = 10$. Thus, the p that will be printed is $p = 10$, which implies the correct answer is (C). ■

Question 3.7. —————————————————————————
Note that one of the *Pythagorean identities* is $\sin^2 x + \cos^2 x = 1$. Hence, the set $\{(\sin t, \cos t) : -\pi/2 \leq t \leq 0\}$ is part of a circle of radius 1. From the unit-circle in precalculus, we know

$$-1 \leq \sin t \leq 0 \quad \text{and} \quad 0 \leq \cos t \leq 1,$$

when $-\pi/2 \leq t \leq 0$, so the graph is in the second quadrant. The only option that satisfies these criteria is (B). ■

Question 3.8.

This is a simple u-substitution. Let $u = 1 + x^2$. Then $du = 2x\,dx$. Hence,

$$
\begin{aligned}
\int_0^1 \frac{x}{1+x^2}\,dx &= \frac{1}{2} \int_0^1 \frac{2x}{1+x^2}\,dx \\
&= \frac{1}{2} \int_{x=0}^1 \frac{du}{u} \\
&= \frac{1}{2} \int_{u=1}^2 \frac{du}{u} \\
&= \frac{1}{2} \log|u| \,\Big|_1^2 \\
&= \frac{1}{2} \left(\log|2| - \log|1| \right) \\
&= \frac{1}{2} \log 2 \\
&= \log \sqrt{2}.
\end{aligned}
$$

It follows that (E) is correct. Lists of *antiderivatives* and *logarithm properties* are in the glossary. ∎

Question 3.9.

The number of one-to-one functions $f : S \to S$ is simply the number of permutations of the list $(1,\ 2,\ 3, \ldots, k)$, which is $k!$. Fill in the bubble for (A). ∎

Question 3.10.

The function g is continuous at a if and only if

$$
\lim_{x \to a} g(x) = g(a),
$$

or equivalently if and only if

$$
\lim_{n \to \infty} g(a_n) = g(a)
$$

for every sequence $\{a_n\}_{n=1}^\infty$ such that $a_n \to a$ as $n \to \infty$.

Let $\{q_n\}_{n=1}^{\infty}$ be a rational sequence such that $q_n \to a$ and let $\{y_n\}_{n=1}^{\infty}$ be an irrational sequence such that $y_n \to a$ as $n \to \infty$. Then

$$\lim_{n \to \infty} g(q_n) = 1 \quad \text{and} \quad \lim_{n \to \infty} g(y_n) = e^a.$$

It follows that g could only be continuous at a when $e^a = 1$. This only occurs when $a = 0$.

Clearly, g is, in fact, continuous at 0, because

$$\lim_{x \to 0} g(x) = 1 = g(0).$$

We select (B). ■

Question 3.11. ───────────────────────

Suppose $x \geq y$. Then $x - y \geq 0$, so $|x - y| = x - y$. It follows that

$$\frac{x + y + |x - y|}{2} = \frac{x + y + x - y}{2} = x.$$

Since $|x - y| = |-(y - x)| = |y - x|$, a nearly identical argument shows that

$$\frac{x + y + |x - y|}{2} = y,$$

when $y > x$.

We conclude that $(x + y + |x - y|)/2$ is the maximum of x and y. As a result, (A) is the correct answer. ■

Question 3.12. ───────────────────────────────

Suppose $B = (0, 1)$. Then B doesn't contain its upper bound of 1. This example disproves all of the options except (C), because ...

(A) B isn't closed.

(B) B is open.

(D) all the terms of $\left\{ 1 - \dfrac{1}{n+1} \right\}_{n=1}^{\infty}$ are in B and the sequence converges to 1.

(E) since 1 is a limit point of B, every open interval containing 1 has some points in B.

By the process of elimination, we conclude that (C) is the right answer. However, we're not being timed, so let's prove it! Suppose b is not a limit point of B. Then there is some $r > 0$ such that the open ball, with center b and radius r, contains no points of B. It's clear that $b - r/2$ is in our ball, but it is less than b and still greater than every value in B. This is a contradiction of the definition of a least upper bound. It follows that every open ball with center b has points in B. So, b is a limit point. ∎

Question 3.13. ───────────────────────────────

Probability properties tells us that for events A and B in the sample space

$$P(A \cup B) = P(A) + P(B) - P(A \cap B),$$

or with C also an event in the sample space

$$P(A \cup B \cup C) = P(A) + P(B \cup C) - P(A \cap (B \cup C))$$

$$= P(A) + P(B) + P(C) - P(B \cap C) - \Big(P(A \cap B)$$

$$+ P(A \cap C) - P(A \cap B \cap C) \Big)$$

$$= P(A) + P(B) + P(C) - P(A \cap B) - P(A \cap C)$$
$$- P(B \cap C) + P(A \cap B \cap C).$$

In our case, getting two blue, two red, or two yellow socks is mutually exclusive, so

$$P(A \cap B) = P(A \cap C) = P(B \cap C) = P(A \cap B \cap C) = 0.$$

The probabilities of picking two blue, two red, and two yellow socks are

$$\frac{2}{8} \cdot \frac{1}{7} = \frac{1}{28}, \quad \frac{4}{8} \cdot \frac{3}{7} = \frac{6}{28}, \quad \text{and} \quad \frac{2}{8} \cdot \frac{1}{7} = \frac{1}{28},$$

respectively.

Therefore, the probability of picking two socks of the same color is

$$\frac{1}{28} + \frac{6}{28} + \frac{1}{28} = \frac{2}{7}.$$

Shade in the bubble for (A). ∎

Question 3.14.

In general, the negation of *For each A there exists B such that C* is *There exists A such that for each B not C*. This can be proven with a truth-table. Furthermore, the negation of *If D, then E* is *D and not E*. Thus, the negation of

> For each s in $\mathbb{R}$, there exists an r in $\mathbb{R}$ such that if $f(r) > 0$, then $g(s) > 0$

must be

> There exists s in $\mathbb{R}$ such that for each r in $\mathbb{R}$ $f(r) > 0$ and $g(s) \not> 0$.

Since $\not>$ is the same as $\leq$, we conclude that the answer is (C). ∎

Question 3.15.

Let's go through the ones that are false first. Choice (A) is wrong. Since $a < g(x) < x$ for x in the interval (a, b), the function g is bounded between a and b. Choice (C) is an untruth. If $a < b < 0$, then the assumptions imply that g would be negative for x in the interval (a, b). Choice (D) and (E) are debunked via the diagram

101

below, which meets all the criteria specified in the question but is neither strictly increasing nor a polynomial of degree 1.

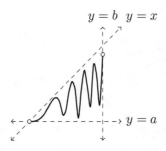

We have already provided enough information to conclude (B) is correct, but let's prove it since the clock isn't ticking down. Suppose $g(x) = k$, where k is a constant. By the stated hypotheses, $a < g(x) = k < x$. Therefore, $(a+k)/2$ is in the open interval (a, b) because it's between a and k. However,

$$g\left(\frac{a+k}{2}\right) = k \not< \frac{a+k}{2},$$

which contradicts the criteria required for g. ∎

Question 3.16. ————————————————————————
If $(1, 2, m, 5)$ is a linear combination of $(0, 1, 1, 1)$, $(0, 0, 0, 1)$, and $(1, 1, 2, 0)$, then there exist c_1, c_2, and c_3 such that

$$c_1(0, 1, 1, 1) + c_2(0, 0, 0, 1) + c_3(1, 1, 2, 0) = (1, 2, m, 5).$$

Rewriting our row vectors as column vectors, and placing them in a matrix gives us

$$\begin{pmatrix} 0 & 0 & 1 \\ 1 & 0 & 1 \\ 1 & 0 & 2 \\ 1 & 1 & 0 \end{pmatrix} \begin{pmatrix} c_1 \\ c_2 \\ c_3 \end{pmatrix} = \begin{pmatrix} 1 \\ 2 \\ m \\ 5 \end{pmatrix}.$$

As an augmented matrix, our equation becomes

$$\begin{pmatrix} 0 & 0 & 1 & | & 1 \\ 1 & 0 & 1 & | & 2 \\ 1 & 0 & 2 & | & m \\ 1 & 1 & 0 & | & 5 \end{pmatrix}.$$

Row reducing yields

$$\begin{pmatrix} 1 & 0 & 1 & | & 2 \\ 0 & 1 & -1 & | & 3 \\ 0 & 0 & 1 & | & m-2 \\ 0 & 0 & 0 & | & 3-m \end{pmatrix}.$$

Thus, $m = 3$. All other m's would lead to the contradiction $0 = 3 - m$. This means (D) is correct. ∎

Question 3.17. ─────────────────────────────
A little algebra shows $f(x+1) = f(x) + \Delta f(x)$ and $\Delta f(x+1) = \Delta f(x) + \Delta^2 f(x)$. Hence,

$$f(2) = f(1) + \Delta f(1) \qquad\qquad f(3) = f(2) + \Delta f(2)$$
$$= -1 + 4 \qquad\qquad\qquad\quad = 3 - 2$$
$$= 3, \qquad\qquad\qquad\qquad\quad = 1,$$

and

$$f(4) = f(3) + \Delta f(3)$$
$$= 1 + \Delta f(2) + \Delta^2 f(2)$$
$$= 1 - 2 + 6$$
$$= 5$$

This result corresponds to option (E). ∎

Question 3.18. ───────────────────────────────────────

It's clear $A(r) = \pi(1 - r^2)$ and $a(r) = \pi(1 - r)^2$. Thus,

$$\lim_{r \to 1^-} \frac{A(r)}{a(r)} = \lim_{r \to 1^-} \frac{\pi(1 - r^2)}{\pi(1 - r)^2}$$
$$= \lim_{r \to 1^-} \frac{1 + r}{1 - r}$$
$$= \infty.$$

Choose (E)! ∎

Question 3.19. ───────────────────────────────────────

Cayley table I is a *group*. It's clear I is closed under our binary operation and a is the identity element. Careful examination shows that I has identity element a and is generated by b: $b^2 = c$, $b^3 = d$, and $b^4 = a$. So, every element has an inverse; b^m has an inverse of b^{4-m} for $m = 0, 1, 2$, and 3. Associativity holds trivially.

Cayley table II is not a group because associativity fails. Consider $(d \cdot c) \cdot c = c$ and $d \cdot (c \cdot c) = d$. To make a quick tip for test takers: Checking associativity case by case takes too long. Instead, notice that the identity element a is listed twice in row c. This is impossible because it means c has two inverses which never happens in groups, so the Cayley table must fail some axiom. Stopping there seems to be consistent with best test taking practices.

Lastly, Cayley table III is not a group. It's clear a is the identity element for III. However, there is no a in row c, which means c has no inverse.

The answer must be (B). ∎

Question 3.20. ───────────────────────────────────────

Let's go through each option. Property I is true, because

$$\lim_{x \to 0} \frac{f(x)}{x} = \lim_{x \to 0} \frac{f(0 + x) - 0}{x} = \lim_{x \to 0} \frac{f(0 + x) - f(0)}{x},$$

which is precisely the definition of the derivative at $x = 0$. Property II is false. Consider $f(x) = x$:

$$\lim_{x \to 0} \frac{x}{x} = \lim_{x \to 0} 1 = 1.$$

Property III must be true, because

$$\lim_{x \to 0} f(x) = \lim_{x \to 0} x \cdot \frac{f(x)}{x} = 0 \cdot L = 0.$$

Since I and III are true and II is false, (D) is correct. ∎

Question 3.21. ─────────────────────────────────────

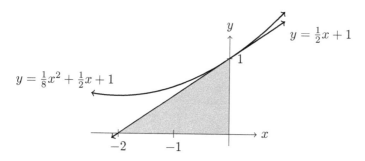

We need to find the equation of the tangent line. The point of tangency is $(0, 1)$, so we just need to find the slope of $y = x^2/8 + x/2 + 1$ at $x = 0$. It's clear

$$y' = \frac{x}{4} + \frac{1}{2} \quad \text{implies} \quad y'\big|_{x=0} = \frac{1}{2}.$$

Hence, the slope of the tangent line must be $1/2$, because this is the slope of $y = x^2/8 + x/2 + 1$ at the point of tangency. It follows that our tangent line is $y = x/2 + 1$.

Graphing shows that the region bounded by the x-axis, y-axis, and the tangent line is a triangle with base 2 and height 1. Therefore, its area must be $(2)(1)/2 = 1$. The correct answer has to be (D). ∎

Question 3.22. —————————————————————————
The set of non-negative integers is not a *group* because it does not have additive inverses for nonzero elements. For example, the additive inverse of 1, i.e. -1, is not in $\{n \in \mathbb{Z} : n \geq 0\}$. Hence, the set of non-negative integers cannot be a subgroup either, so we pick (B). ∎

Question 3.23. —————————————————————————
Consider the diagram shown below, and in particular $\triangle BAO$.

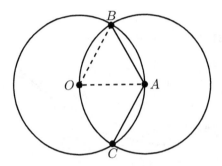

It's clear $AB = AO = BO$. Since the lengths of the sides are the same, it must be the case that

$$\text{angle } AOB \cong \text{angle } ABO \cong \text{angle } OAB.$$

It follows that each angle must have a measure of 60°. By symmetry, the measure of angle $OAC = 60°$. Therefore, the measure of angle $BAC = 120°$. As a result, choice (C) is correct. ∎

Question 3.24. ————————————————————————

See the glossary for a definition of a *basis*. Suppose $x := (x_1, x_2, x_3, x_4)$ is orthogonal to both $(0, 1, 1, 1)$ and $(1, 1, 1, 0)$. Because the dot product of two orthogonal vectors is 0,

$$x \cdot (0, 1, 1, 1) = x_2 + x_3 + x_4 \quad \text{and} \quad x \cdot (1, 1, 1, 0) = x_1 + x_2 + x_3$$
$$= 0 \qquad\qquad\qquad\qquad\qquad\qquad\qquad = 0.$$

A bit of arithmetic shows that

$$x_1 = x_4 \quad \text{and} \quad x_2 = -x_3 - x_4,$$

where both x_3 and x_4 are free. Hence, any vector of the form

$$\begin{aligned} x &= (-x_4, -x_3 - x_4, x_3, x_4) \\ &= (0, -x_3, x_3, 0) + (-x_4, -x_4, 0, x_4) \\ &= x_3(0, -1, 1, 0) + x_4(1, -1, 0, 1) \end{aligned}$$

is orthogonal to our two vectors, so $\{(0, -1, 1, 0), (1, -1, 0, 1)\}$ is an orthogonal basis. Since all finite bases for a vector space have the same number of elements, our basis must have two elements too, which narrows our choices down to (B) and (C). It cannot be (B) because $(1, 1, 1, 0) \cdot (1, 0, 0, 0) \neq 0$.

Another approach is as follows.

(1) Examine what choices are consistent with a basis, leaving (A), (B), and (C).

(2) Check the orthogonality between the potential bases' elements and our vectors one-by-one, leaving (A) and (C).

(3) Of the remaining choices pick the set with the most elements, specifically (C).

This process takes more or less the same amount of time as the solution described above, but checking linear independence, which is required for (1), is often time-consuming when dealing with more than two vectors. ∎

Question 3.25.

According to the *Extreme value theorem*, f has an absolute maximum because f is real-valued and its domain is *compact*. The maximum will be on the boundary or at a relative maximum. From Calculus, we know that relative extrema occur when the partial derivatives are undefined or zero. But $f_x(x,y) = 5$ and $f_y(x,y) = -4$, so f has no relative extrema. Hence, the maximum of f must be on the boundary.

Let's graph the domain of f.

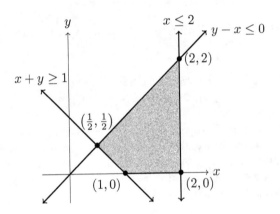

Suppose $y = x$. Then $f(x,x) = x$ and $1/2 \leq x \leq 2$. Therefore, $f(2,2) = 2$ is the maximum value of f on $y = x$.

Assume $y = 1 - x$. Then $f(x, 1-x) = 5x - 4(1-x) = 9x - 4$ and $1/2 \leq x \leq 1$. Therefore, $f(1,0) = 5$ is the maximum value of f on $y = 1 - x$.

Say $y = 0$. Then $f(x,0) = 5x$ and $1 \leq x \leq 2$. Therefore, $f(2,0) = 10$ is the maximum on $y = 0$.

The last boundary is $x = 2$, which implies $f(2,y) = 10 - 4y$ and $0 \leq y \leq 2$. It's clear that $y = 0$ maximizes f on this boundary and $f(2,0) = 10$.

We conclude that the absolute maximum value of f on the domain specified is 10. This implies (D) is correct. ∎

Question 3.26. ⸻

Extrapolating from the *Extreme value theorem*, it's clear that absolute extrema occur at relative extrema or else

$$\lim_{x \to -\infty} f(x) \quad \text{and} \quad \lim_{x \to -\infty} f(x)$$

will be values greater or smaller than f at our relative extrema. Let's compute the pieces.

We have

$$\lim_{x \to \infty} f(x) = \lim_{x \to \infty} -x^2 + 2 \quad \text{and} \quad \lim_{x \to -\infty} f(x) = \lim_{x \to -\infty} -x^2 + 4x - 2$$

$$= -\infty \qquad\qquad\qquad\qquad\qquad = -\infty.$$

We need the derivative of f, so we can find our critical numbers. It's not too hard to see

$$f'(x) = \begin{cases} -2x + 4 & \text{if } x < 1, \\ -2x & \text{if } x > 1. \end{cases}$$

Note in particular that $x = 1$ is a critical number since $f'(1)$ is undefined because

$$\lim_{x \to 1^-} f'(x) = 2 \quad \text{and} \quad \lim_{x \to 1^+} f'(x) = -2.$$

This is because *derivatives have no "simple discontinuities"*, i.e. the left and right limits of a derivative agree if they both exist. It's clear f' has no other critical numbers, because $-2x + 4$ is never zero when $x < 1$ and $-2x$ is never zero when $x > 1$.

It follows that there $f(1) = 1$ is our absolute maximum, since it is the only relative extremum and $f(x) \to -\infty$ as $|x| \to \infty$. Fill in the bubble for (B). ∎

Question 3.27.
This is tricky if you overthink it. However, obtaining the answer is quite trivial. If $f(x) = f(1-x)$ for all x, then

$$\frac{d}{dx}\left(f(x) \right) = \frac{d}{dx}\left(f(1-x) \right) \quad \text{implies} \quad f'(x) = -f'(1-x).$$

Evaluating at $x = 0$ shows

$$f'(0) = -f'(1).$$

This result corresponds to (E). ∎

Question 3.28.
This reduces to an equivalent problem with *bases*, since every subspace has a basis and the number of elements in a basis is its dimension. Consider a basis for $V_1 \cap V_2$ and extend it to a basis for V_1 Call it $\mathcal{B}_1$. Extend $\mathcal{B}_1 \cap V_2$ to a basis of V_2 and call it $\mathcal{B}_2$. The set $\mathcal{B}_1 \cap \mathcal{B}_2$ is a basis for $V_1 \cap V_2$, because we built $\mathcal{B}_2$ from $\mathcal{B}_1 \cap V_2$. Extend $\mathcal{B}_1 \cup \mathcal{B}_2$ to a basis of V, and call it $\mathcal{B}$. The *inclusion-exclusion principle* implies

$$|\mathcal{B}_1 \cup \mathcal{B}_2| = |\mathcal{B}_1| + |\mathcal{B}_2| - |\mathcal{B}_1 \cap \mathcal{B}_2| = 12 - |\mathcal{B}_1 \cap \mathcal{B}_2|.$$

Since $\mathcal{B}_1 \cup \mathcal{B}_2 \subseteq \mathcal{B}$,

$$
\begin{aligned}
12 - |\mathcal{B}_1 \cap \mathcal{B}_2| &\le |\mathcal{B}| \\
\Rightarrow \quad 12 - |\mathcal{B}_1 \cap \mathcal{B}_2| &\le 10 \\
\Rightarrow \quad |\mathcal{B}_1 \cap \mathcal{B}_2| &\ge 2.
\end{aligned}
$$

We conclude that the smallest possible dimension of $V_1 \cap V_2$ is 2, and we select (C). ∎

Question 3.29. ———————————————————————————

We will use *integration by parts*. Let $u = x$ and $dv = p''(x)\ dx$. Then $du = dx$ and $v = p'(x)$. Therefore,

$$\int_0^2 xp''(x)\ dx = xp'(x) - \int p'(x)\ dx \bigg|_0^2$$

$$= xp'(x) - p(x) \bigg|_0^2$$

$$= 2p'(2) - p(2) + p(0)$$

$$= 2(-1) - 3 + 3$$

$$= -2.$$

We conclude that (B) is correct. ∎

Question 3.30. ———————————————————————————

Choice (A) is false. Suppose $\mathbf{0}$ is in $\mathcal{B}$. Since the dimension of V is greater than 1, there is another vector $v \neq \mathbf{0}$ in $\mathcal{B}$. But $0v = \mathbf{0}$, which contradicts the fact that the elements of a *basis* are linearly independent.

Choice (B) is an untruth. Suppose the elements of $\mathcal{A}$ span V and $\mathcal{A} \subset \mathcal{B}$. Choose v in $\mathcal{B} \setminus \mathcal{A}$. Because $\mathcal{B} \subset V$,

$$v = c_1 v_1 + c_2 v_2 + \ldots + c_n v_n$$

for some v_i in $\mathcal{A}$ and c_i in the underlying field $\mathbb{F}$. This contradicts linear independence of $\mathcal{B}$, because $\mathcal{A}$ is a subset of $\mathcal{B}$.

Choice (C) is impossible. Suppose $\mathcal{B} \subset \mathcal{C}$, where $\mathcal{C}$ is a linearly independent subset of V. Choose v in $\mathcal{C} \setminus \mathcal{B}$. Since $\mathcal{B}$ is a basis of V, there exist $c_1, c_2, \ldots c_n$ in the underlying field $\mathbb{F}$ and $v_1, v_2, \ldots, v_n$ in $\mathcal{B}$ such that

$$v = c_1 v_1 + c_2 v_2 + \ldots + c_n v_n.$$

But this contradicts linear independence of $\mathcal{C}$ because $\mathcal{B}$ is a subset of $\mathcal{C}$.

Choice (E) cannot possibly be true. It directly contradicts the linear independence criterion of a basis.

Thus, choice (D) must be correct. As we know from the remarks above **0** is not in $\mathcal{B}$. Hence, $\mathcal{D} := \{2v : v \in \mathcal{B}\}$ could be disjoint from $\mathcal{B}$ and still be a basis for V. We emphasize the keyword *could*; our example doesn't work if the underlying field has characteristic 2. ■

Question 3.31.

Recall the *Rational roots theorem*:

> Suppose $p(x) = a_n x^n + a_{n-1} x^{n-1} + \ldots + a_0$ is a polynomial such that $a_1, a_2, \ldots, a_n$ are integers. Then every rational root can be reduced to p/q, where p is an integer factor of a_0 and q is an integer factor of a_n.

Not much can be said about the numerator of a rational root of $9x^5 + ax^3 + b$ because we don't know the value of b, but the denominator must be a factor of 9. Four does not meet this criterion so $1/4$ cannot be a root. It follows that (C) is correct. ■

Question 3.32.

The total number of ways 20 children can be lined up is 20!, half of which have Pat behind Lynn and half have Pat ahead of Lynn. Thus, the total number of combinations with Pat ahead of Lynn is $20!/2$. Choose (D) and continue! ■

Question 3.33.

There are a total of $\lfloor \frac{1,000}{30} \rfloor = \lfloor 33.\overline{3} \rfloor = 33$ integers from 1 to 1,000 that are divisible by 30. A number is divisible by both 30 and 16 if and only if it is divisible by their least common multiple 240. There are a total of $\lfloor \frac{1,000}{240} \rfloor = \lfloor 4.1\overline{6} \rfloor = 4$ numbers from 1 to 1,000 divisible by 240. We conclude that there are a total of $33 - 4 = 29$ integers from 1 to 1,000 that are divisible by 30 but not 16. Shade the bubble for (A). ■

112

Question 3.34. ─────────────────────────────────

Choice (B) is not always true. The function f may not have a second derivative, and even if it does $\lim_{x \to \infty} f''(x)$ may not exist. Consider

$$f(x) := \int_1^{x^2} \frac{\sin t^2}{t^2} \, dt.$$

The second derivative of f is

$$f''(x) = 8 \cos x^4 - \frac{6 \sin x^4}{x^4},$$

which does not converge to a particular value as $x \to \infty$.

The necessity of choices (C), (D), and (E) is easily disproven by

$$f(x) := 1 - e^{-x}.$$

The correct answer must be (A). Let's prove it, since we're not on the clock. Suppose

$$\lim_{x \to \infty} f(x) = L_0 \quad \text{and} \quad \lim_{x \to \infty} f'(x) = L_1.$$

By assumption, L_0 and L_1 are finite. We want to prove $L_1 = 0$. Due to the definition of a limit for every sequence $\{c_n\}_{n=1}^{\infty}$ such that $\lim_{n \to \infty} c_n = \infty$ we have $\lim_{n \to \infty} f'(c_n) = L_1$. So, $\lim_{n \to \infty} f'(c_n) = L_1$ for any particular sequence $\{c_n\}_{n=1}^{\infty}$ such that $\lim_{n \to \infty} c_n = \infty$. Define c_n to be a number in interval $(n, n+1)$ such that

$$f'(c_n) = \frac{f(n+1) - f(n)}{n+1-n} = f(n+1) - f(n).$$

We are guarantied that c_n exists for all n because of the Mean value theorem. Furthermore, it's clear $\lim_{n \to \infty} c_n = \infty$. Thus,

$$L_1 = \lim_{x \to \infty} f'(x) = \lim_{n \to \infty} f'(c_n) = \lim_{n \to \infty} f(n+1) - f(n).$$

Since $\lim_{x \to \infty} f(x) = L_0$, we know $f(n)$ and $f(n+1)$ tend to L_0 as $n \to \infty$. Thus,

$$L_1 = L_0 - L_0 = 0.$$

■

Question 3.35. ————————————————————————
To find the equation of a plane, we need two vectors. A vector normal to the plane, and a vector parallel to the plane which contains an arbitrary point (x, y, z) of the plane.

We will find a normal vector first. If our plane is tangent to the surface $z = e^{-x} \sin y$ at $x = 0$ and $y = \pi/2$, then it has the same normal vector n at this point. From Calculus, we know a normal vector to the plane described by $z = f(x, y)$ is

$$n = \left(f_x(x, y), f_y(x, y), -1 \right).$$

Let's compute the pieces:

$$f_x\left(0, \frac{\pi}{2}\right) = -e^{-0} \sin \frac{\pi}{2} \quad \text{and} \quad f_y\left(0, \frac{\pi}{2}\right) = e^{-0} \cos \frac{\pi}{2}$$
$$= -1 \qquad\qquad\qquad\qquad = 0.$$

Hence, $n := (-1, 0, -1)$ is normal to our plane.

The next piece of information we need is a vector parallel to our plane. When $x = 0$ and $y = \pi/2$,

$$z = e^{-0} \sin \frac{\pi}{2} = 1.$$

Therefore, $(0, \pi/2, 1)$ is on our plane. It follows that the vector $v := (x, y - \pi/2, z - 1)$ is parallel to our plane, whenever (x, y, z) is a point on our plane.

We know that the dot product of v and n is 0, because the vectors are orthogonal. So,

$$v \cdot n = -x + 0 \left(y - \frac{\pi}{2} \right) - (z - 1) = 0.$$

Thus,

$$x + z = 1$$

is an equation of the plane tangent to the surface $z = e^{-x} \sin y$ at the point where $x = 0$ and $y = \pi/2$. This result implies (B) is correct. ∎

Question 3.36. ———————————————————————

It's clear

$$\mu(x) = \frac{4 + 5 + 7 + 9 + x}{5} = \frac{25 + x}{5},$$

for all x. The median function is a little more tricky:

$$\eta(x) = \begin{cases} 7 & \text{if } x \geq 7, \\ x & \text{if } 5 \leq x < 7, \\ 5 & \text{if } x < 5. \end{cases}$$

All that is left is to analyze what happens to η in each of its three cases:

Suppose $x \geq 7$ and $\mu(x) = \eta(x)$. Then

$$\frac{25 + x}{5} = 7.$$

This implies $x = 10$.

Let $5 \leq x < 7$ and $\mu(x) = \eta(x)$. Then

$$\frac{25 + x}{5} = x.$$

This implies $x = 6.25$.

Assume $x < 5$ and $\mu(x) = \eta(x)$. Then

$$\frac{25 + x}{5} = 5.$$

This implies $x = 0$.

Thus, there is a total of three values of x that satisfy the criteria described in the question, which means (D) is to be selected. ∎

Question 3.37. ———————————————————————

Recall

$$e := \sum_{n=0}^{\infty} \frac{1}{n!}.$$

Knowing the above, the problem may still be difficult, but it is now no more than a matter of rearranging, simplifying, and reindexing. Call the sum S. Then

$$S = \sum_{k=1}^{\infty} \frac{k^2}{k!} = \sum_{k=1}^{\infty} \frac{k}{(k-1)!}.$$

Let $m = k - 1$. So,

$$S = \sum_{m=0}^{\infty} \frac{m+1}{m!}$$

$$= \sum_{m=0}^{\infty} \frac{m}{m!} + \sum_{m=0}^{\infty} \frac{1}{m!}$$

$$= \left(0 + \sum_{m=1}^{\infty} \frac{1}{(m-1)!}\right) + \sum_{m=0}^{\infty} \frac{1}{m!}$$

$$= \sum_{m=1}^{\infty} \frac{1}{(m-1)!} + \sum_{m=0}^{\infty} \frac{1}{m!}.$$

Notice that if $n = m - 1$, the first sum becomes $\sum_{n=0}^{\infty} \frac{1}{n!}$ which is equal to the second sum $\sum_{m=0}^{\infty} \frac{1}{m!}$. Hence,

$$S = 2 \sum_{n=0}^{\infty} \frac{1}{n!} = 2e.$$

Pick (B)! ■

Question 3.38. ———————————————————————

One of the basic *integration properties* from Calculus is that if f and g are integrable and $f \leq g$ on the closed interval $[a, b]$ then

$$\int_a^b f(x)\, dx \leq \int_a^b g(x)\, dx.$$

116

Also, note that $\sin t$ and $\cos t$ are non-negative when t is in $[0, \pi/2]$. Let's examine our integrands. It's clear

$$\sin t \leq \cos t$$

on $[0, \pi/4]$. It's also true that

$$\cos 2t \leq \cos t$$

for t in $[0, \pi/4]$, because $\cos t$ is monotonically decreasing when t is in $[0, \pi/2]$ and the graph of $\cos 2t$ is the graph of $\cos t$ compressed horizontally to half of its original length. Lastly, both

$$\cos^2 t \leq \cos t \quad \text{and} \quad \sin t \cos t \leq \cos t,$$

because $0 \leq \sin t \leq 1$ and $0 \leq \cos t \leq 1$ when t is in $[0, \pi/4]$. It follows that (B) is correct. ∎

Question 3.39.

Notice all these options, except (E), are—in some sense—describing the area between e^{-x} and x-axis when $0 \leq x \leq 10$. Let $\mathcal{R} :=$ $\{(x, y) : 0 \leq x \leq 10, 0 \leq y \leq e^{-x}\}$.

Choice (A) is an approximation of the area of $\mathcal{R}$ using n rectangles. The j-th rectangle has width $x_j - x_{j-1}$ and height $f(x_j)$, i.e. the height of the j-th rectangle is f evaluated at the right endpoint of the j-th interval.

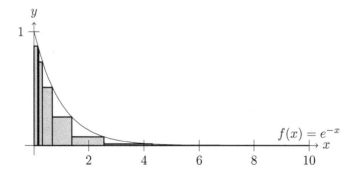

Choice (B) is an approximation of the area of $\mathcal{R}$ using n rectangles. The j-th rectangle has width $x_j - x_{j-1}$ and height $f(x_{j-1})$, i.e. the height of the j-th rectangle is f evaluated at the left endpoint of the j-th interval.

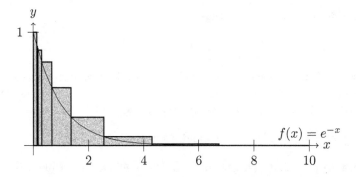

Choice (C) is an approximation of the area of $\mathcal{R}$ using n rectangles. The j-th rectangle has width $x_j - x_{j-1}$ and height $f\left(\frac{x_j + x_{j-1}}{2}\right)$, i.e. the height of the j-th rectangle is f evaluated at the midpoint of the j-th interval.

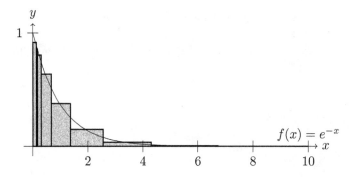

Choice (D) is the actual area of $\mathcal{R}$.

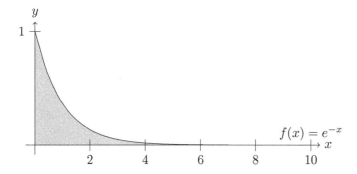

Choice (E) is clearly out because the area of $\mathcal{R}$ is greater than 0.

As the graphs above make clear, (B) is the correct answer. Generally, when f is monotonically decreasing, using the value of x at the left endpoint of each interval for the height of the rectangle is an overestimate of the area under the curve. ■

Question 3.40. ───────────────────────────

Coin tosses are an example of a *binomial distribution*. We need the following formula.

> Suppose we have a binomial distribution and the probability of one successful trial is p. Then the probability of exactly k successes in n independent trials is
>
> $$\binom{n}{k} p^k (1-p)^{n-k}.$$

Suppose a success is getting heads. Our task is to compute the probability that the number of heads k is greater than or equal to 5. There are a total of $n = 8$ trials and the probability of each trial ending in success is $p = 1/2$. Thus, using the above formula and basic *probability properties* it follows that this event

119

has probability

$$\binom{8}{5}\left(\frac{1}{2}\right)^8 + \binom{8}{6}\left(\frac{1}{2}\right)^8 + \binom{8}{7}\left(\frac{1}{2}\right)^8 + \binom{8}{8}\left(\frac{1}{2}\right)^8$$

$$= \frac{1}{256}\left(\binom{8}{5} + \binom{8}{6} + \binom{8}{7} + \binom{8}{8}\right)$$

$$= \frac{1}{256}\left(\frac{8!}{3!5!} + \frac{8!}{2!6!} + \frac{8!}{1!7!} + \frac{8!}{0!8!}\right)$$

$$= \frac{1}{256}(56 + 28 + 8 + 1)$$

$$= \frac{93}{256}.$$

Select (E)! ■

Question 3.41. ─────────────────────────────
We will use *second derivatives test* from Calculus.

Suppose that the function $f : \mathbb{R}^2 \to \mathbb{R}$ has continuous second order partial derivatives in some $E \subseteq \mathbb{R}^2$. Suppose the point (a, b) in E is a critical point, i.e. $f_x(a, b) = 0$ and $f_y(a, b) = 0$. Define

$$H_f(x, y) := \det\begin{pmatrix} f_{xx}(x,y) & f_{xy}(x,y) \\ f_{yx}(x,y) & f_{yy}(x,y) \end{pmatrix}$$

$$= f_{xx}(x, y)f_{yy}(x, y) - (f_{xy}(x, y))^2.$$

- If $f_{xx}(a, b) > 0$ and $H_f(a, b) > 0$, then $f(a, b)$ is a relative minimum.

- If $f_{xx}(a, b) < 0$ and $H_f(a, b) > 0$, then $f(a, b)$ is a relative maximum.

- If $H_f(a, b) < 0$, then (a, b) is a saddle point.

- If $H_f(a, b) = 0$, then the test gives no information.

Let's compute our critical numbers. It's clear

$$f_x(x, y) = y - 3x^2 \quad \text{and} \quad f_y(x, y) = x - 3y^2.$$

120

Setting our partials equal to zero, and solving shows that our critical points are $(0,0)$ and $(1/3, 1/3)$.

Next, we compute our second order partial derivatives, which we will use to find our relative maximum:

$$f_{xx}(x,y) = -6x, \quad f_{xy}(x,y) = 1, \quad f_{yx}(x,y) = 1, \text{ and } \quad f_{yy}(x,y) = -6y,$$

which implies

$$H_f(x,y) = 36xy - 1.$$

It follows that

$$f_{xx}\left(\frac{1}{3}, \frac{1}{3}\right) = -2 < 0 \quad \text{and} \quad H_f\left(\frac{1}{3}, \frac{1}{3}\right) = 3 > 0.$$

Therefore, there is a relative maximum at $(1/3, 1/3)$, so we choose (E). Note: $H_f(0,0) = -1$, which means there is a saddle point when $x = y = 0$. ■

Question 3.42.
This is tricky because C is so far from the origin in the southeast direction, that it makes our graph too large to manage. To alleviate this issue, let's scale our points by $1/2$ before we graph them, i.e. let's graph $A' = (-1/2, 1)$, $B' = (3, 2)$, and $C' = (1/2, -10)$. Since angles are preserved under contractions, this will not affect the result.

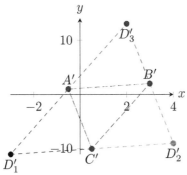

In case it's hard to see, our parallelograms are $\square A'D_1'C'B'$, $\square A'C'D_2'B'$, and $\square A'C'B'D_3'$. We conclude that (D) is correct. ■

121

Question 3.43. ────────────────────────────

After a quick glance, it's easy to that

$$\begin{pmatrix} 6 \\ 7 \\ 8 \end{pmatrix} = -\begin{pmatrix} 0 \\ 1 \\ 2 \end{pmatrix} + 2\begin{pmatrix} 3 \\ 4 \\ 5 \end{pmatrix}.$$

Since matrices are linear transformations,

$$A\begin{pmatrix} 6 \\ 7 \\ 8 \end{pmatrix} = A\left(-\begin{pmatrix} 0 \\ 1 \\ 2 \end{pmatrix} + 2\begin{pmatrix} 3 \\ 4 \\ 5 \end{pmatrix}\right)$$

$$= -A\begin{pmatrix} 0 \\ 1 \\ 2 \end{pmatrix} + 2A\begin{pmatrix} 3 \\ 4 \\ 5 \end{pmatrix}$$

$$= -\begin{pmatrix} 1 \\ 0 \\ 0 \end{pmatrix} + 2\begin{pmatrix} 0 \\ 1 \\ 0 \end{pmatrix}$$

$$= \begin{pmatrix} -1 \\ 2 \\ 0 \end{pmatrix}.$$

This result corresponds to (B). ∎

Question 3.44. ────────────────────────────

Choice (A) is true:

$$\lim_{x \to 0^+} (\sqrt{x})^x = \lim_{x \to 0^+} e^{x \log(x)/2}$$

$$= e^{\lim_{x \to 0^+} \frac{\log x}{2/x}}$$

$$\overset{LH}{=} e^{\lim_{x \to 0^+} -x/2}$$

$$= 1.$$

We denote *L'Hôspital's rule* with an *LH* above.

Choice (B) is clearly sound, because $(\sqrt{x})^x > \sqrt{x}$ when $x > 1$ and $\sqrt{x} \to \infty$ as $x \to \infty$.

Choice (C) is valid. It's a simple application of exponent rules; $(\sqrt{x})^x = (x^{1/2})^x = x^{x/2}$. It's only over the complex domain that $x^{1/2}$ is a dubious statement.

Choice (D) is the falsity, which makes it the correct answer. Let's compute the derivative:

$$\frac{d}{dx}\left(x^{x/2}\right) = \frac{d}{dx}\left(e^{x\log(x)/2}\right)$$

$$= e^{x\log(x)/2}\left(\frac{1}{2} + \frac{\log x}{2}\right)$$

$$= x^{x/2}\left(\frac{1}{2} + \frac{\log x}{2}\right).$$

Recall that $\lim_{x\to 0+}\log x = -\infty$. So, it looks like $f'(x) < 0$ for a positive x sufficiently small. Let's try $x = 1/e^2$:

$$\left(\frac{1}{e^2}\right)^{1/2e^2}\left(\frac{1}{2} + \frac{\log(1/e^2)}{2}\right) = \left(\frac{1}{e^2}\right)^{1/2e^2}\left(\frac{1}{2} - \frac{2}{2}\right)$$

$$= -\frac{1}{2}\left(\frac{1}{e^2}\right)^{1/2e^2}$$

$$< 0$$

See the glossary if you have questions on any of the *logarithm properties* utilized.

Choice (E) is true. We've already computed $f'(x)$, so $f''(x)$ is a simple application of the product rule:

$$\frac{d}{dx}\left(x^{x/2}\left(\frac{1}{2} + \frac{\log x}{2}\right)\right) = x^{x/2}\left(\frac{1}{2x}\right) + x^{x/2}\left(\frac{1}{2} + \frac{\log x}{2}\right)^2$$

For $x > 0$, the first term is always positive and the square in the second term guaranties its positivity as well. ∎

Question 3.45.

The function $E(v(t))$ measures the ratio of distance traveled to the amount of fuel used at velocity $v(t)$, so $1/E(v(t))$ must be the ratio of fuel used to distance traveled at velocity $v(t)$. Hence,

$$dG = \frac{ds}{E(v(t))},$$

where dG is the infinitesimal amount of fuel used and ds is an infinitesimal distance traveled. Furthermore,

$$\frac{ds}{dt} = v(t) \quad \text{implies} \quad ds = v(t)\, dt.$$

Therefore,

$$
\begin{aligned}
G &= \int_{t=0}^{4} dG \\
&= \int_{t=0}^{4} \frac{ds}{E(v(t))} \\
&= \int_{0}^{4} \frac{v(t)}{E(v(t))}\, dt.
\end{aligned}
$$

It follows that (A) is correct. ∎

Question 3.46.

If α_1 and α_2 are the two zeros of a monic second-degree polynomial p, then

$$p(x) = (x - \alpha_1)(x - \alpha_2) = x^2 - (\alpha_1 + \alpha_2)x + \alpha_1\alpha_2,$$

so the coefficient of the term of degree 1 is the opposite of the sum of the two zeros. Note "monic" means the coefficient of the term of highest degree is 1.

With this in mind, let's compute the characteristic equation of our matrix:

$$
\begin{aligned}
\det \begin{pmatrix} \lambda - \cos t & -\sin t \\ \sin t & \lambda - \cos t \end{pmatrix} &= (\lambda - \cos t)^2 + \sin^2 t \\
&= \lambda^2 - 2\lambda \cos t + \cos^2 t + \sin^2 t \\
&= \lambda^2 - 2\lambda \cos t + 1.
\end{aligned}
$$

Thus, if $\lambda_1 + \lambda_2 = 1$, then $2\cos t = 1$. This implies $t = \pi/3$. Select (C). See the glossary for a list of *sine and cosine values in quadrant I.* ■

Question 3.47. ⸻
If the distance between x and y is less than $1/2$, then $|x - y| < 1/2$. Since x and y are uniformly distributed independent random variables over a sample space of area 1 the probability that $|x - y| < 1/2$ is simply the area of the region within the sample space where this is true.

Let's graph it! First note that

$$|x - y| < \frac{1}{2} \quad \text{implies} \quad x - \frac{1}{2} < y < x + \frac{1}{2}.$$

So, we draw the dashed lines $y = x - 1/2$ and $y = x + 1/2$, and shade the area between them.

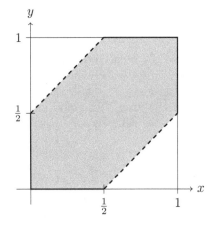

From here, it is easy enough to calculate that the probability is $3/4$. Option (E) must be correct. ■

Question 3.48. ————————————————————————————

The boundary of $\{(x,y) : 0 \leq x \leq 1 \text{ and } 0 \leq y \leq 1\}$ will be sent to the boundary of our new region. With this in mind, our strategy will be to break up the boundary of the region in the xy-plane into four cases and see what boundary is formed in the uv-plane.

Case I $x = 0$: Then $u = y$, $v = 1 + y$, and $0 \leq y \leq 1$, which implies $v = 1 + u$, $0 \leq u \leq 1$, and $1 \leq v \leq 2$.

Case II $y = 0$: Then $u = x^{1/3}$, $v = 1$, and $0 \leq x \leq 1$, which implies $0 \leq u \leq 1$ when $v = 1$.

Case III $x = 1$: Then $u = 1 + y$, $v = 1 + y$, and $0 \leq y \leq 1$, which implies $u = v$, $1 \leq u \leq 2$, and $1 \leq v \leq 2$.

Case IV $y = 1$: Then $u = x^{1/3} + 1$, $v = 2$, and $0 \leq x \leq 1$, which implies $1 \leq u \leq 2$ when $v = 2$.

From here, one can either draw the boundary in the uv-plane or compare our result to the options available. Regardless of which process is chosen, the solution is (A). ∎

Question 3.49. ————————————————————————————

All of these are true, so (E) is correct. The first relationship is true because the graph of $y = f(x - 3)$ is the graph of $y = f(x)$ shifted right 3 units, so integrating over bounds that are also shifted right 3 units doesn't affect the area. We could also prove it with the u-substitution $u = x - 3$. The second relationship follows from *integration properties* since

$$\int_a^3 f(x)\,dx - \int_b^3 f(x)\,dx = \int_a^3 f(x)\,dx + \int_3^b f(x)\,dx$$

$$= \int_a^b f(x)\,dx.$$

The third relationship is true because the graph of $y = f(3x)$ is the graph of $y = f(x)$ compressed horizontally by a factor of 3, so integrating $f(3x)$ over bounds scaled by $1/3$ will give a third the area (we get all the y-values but in a third of the horizontal width). Alternatively, the u-substitution $u = 3x$ proves it. ∎

Question 3.50. ───────────────────────────────

If $(f(x))^2 = x^2$, then $|f(x)| = |x|$ or $f(x) = \pm x$. The arithmetic alone suggests the sign could change at any value of x in the closed interval $[-1, 1]$. However, f must be continuous, which implies that the sign can only change at $x = 0$. This is enough to conclude our functions are

$$f(x) = x, \quad f(x) = -x, \quad f(x) = |x|, \quad \text{and} \quad f(x) = -|x|.$$

This result corresponds to (D). ■

Question 3.51. ───────────────────────────────

From Calculus, we know

$$\sum_{k=1}^{\infty} \frac{(x + 2y)^k}{k}$$

converges when $|x + 2y| < 1$. Let's prove this using the *ratio test*:

$$\lim_{k \to \infty} \left| \frac{\frac{(x+2y)^{k+1}}{k+1}}{\frac{(x+2y)^k}{k}} \right| = \lim_{k \to \infty} \left| \frac{(x+2y)^{k+1}}{k+1} \cdot \frac{k}{(x+2y)^k} \right|$$

$$= \lim_{k \to \infty} \frac{k}{k+1} |x + 2y|$$

$$= |x + 2y|.$$

The ratio test tells us that the series converges when $|x + 2y| < 1$, and the series may or may not converge when $|x+2y| = 1$. However, there is no need to consider the inconclusive case because it would be on the boundary of D.

We have

$$|x + 2y| < 1 \quad \text{implies} \quad -\frac{x+1}{2} < y < -\frac{x-1}{2}.$$

Thus, the interior of D is the open region between the lines $y = -(x+1)/2$ and $y = -(x-1)/2$. These lines both have slope $-1/2$, so they are parallel. We select (D).

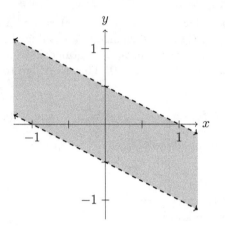

Question 3.52. ─────────────────────────────
First, we convert our system into augmented matrix form, which yields

$$\left(\begin{array}{ccc|c} 1 & 1 & 1 & 0 \\ 1 & 2 & 3 & 0 \\ 1 & 3 & b & 0 \end{array}\right).$$

Using elementary row operations to change our matrix into row-echelon from gives us

$$\left(\begin{array}{ccc|c} 1 & 1 & 1 & 0 \\ 0 & 1 & 2 & 0 \\ 0 & 0 & b-5 & 0 \end{array}\right).$$

From here, it's clear that $b \neq 5$ permits only one solution, and $b = 5$ gives us infinitely many. This means the correct answer is (D). ■

Question 3.53.

We need *Cauchy's residue theorem*.

Suppose U is a simply connected open subset of $\mathbb{C}$ and f a function holomorphic on $U \setminus \{a_1, a_2, \ldots, a_n\}$. Let C be a positively oriented simple closed curve whose graph is contained in U such that $a_1, a_2, \ldots, a_n$ are inside of C. Then

$$\int_C f(z)\, dz = 2\pi i \sum_{k=1}^n \mathrm{Res}(f, a_k),$$

where for a_k a pole of order m

$$\mathrm{Res}(f, a_k) = \frac{1}{(m-1)!} \lim_{z \to a_k} \frac{d^{m-1}}{dz^{m-1}}\left((z - a_k)^m f(z) \right).$$

The rest is an easy computation. The two poles of

$$\frac{1}{(z-1)(z+3)^2}$$

are $z = 1$ and $z = -3$. However, the latter pole is not contained within the circle C. Thus,

$$\int_C \frac{dz}{(z-1)(z+3)^2} = 2\pi i\, \mathrm{Res}(f, 1)$$

$$= 2\pi i \lim_{z \to 1} \frac{1}{(z+3)^2}$$

$$= \frac{\pi i}{8}.$$

Select (D). ∎

Question 3.54. ——————————————————————————
The first step is to set up the differential equation. Since the rate of change of the volume of water in the tank is the rate water enters minus the rate water leaves, we have

$$\frac{dV}{dt} = 1 - 0.25h.$$

Furthermore, since the volume of a rectangular prism is the area of the base times the height, we know $V(t) = 100h(t)$. It follows that

$$\frac{dV}{dt} = 100\frac{dh}{dt} \quad \text{implies} \quad 100\frac{dh}{dt} = 1 - 0.25h.$$

Hence,

$$100\frac{dh}{dt} = 1 - 0.25h$$

$$\Rightarrow \qquad \frac{dh}{h-4} = -0.0025\, dt$$

$$\Rightarrow \qquad \int \frac{dh}{h-4} = -0.0025 \int dt$$

$$\Rightarrow \quad \log|h-4| = -0.0025t + C$$

$$\Rightarrow \qquad h - 4 = \pm e^C \cdot e^{-0.0025t}.$$

It follows that

$$h(t) = Ke^{-0.0025t} + 4,$$

where $K = \pm e^C$. Thus,

$$\lim_{t\to\infty} V(t) = \lim_{t\to\infty} 100h(t)$$

$$= \lim_{t\to\infty} 100\left(Ke^{-0.0025t} + 4\right)$$

$$= 400.$$

This result corresponds to (A).   ∎

Question 3.55. ─────────────────────────────────────

Property I does not apply to f. Because $f'(0)$ is negative and f' is continuous, f is decreasing on some interval starting at $x = 0$.

Property II and III apply to f. We are given that f'' is increasing and has a unique zero, say z_2. Since f'' is always increasing

$$f''(t) \geq f''(z_2 + 1) > 0 \quad \text{when} \quad t \geq z_2 + 1.$$

Due to *integration properties*,

$$\int_{z_2+1}^{x} f''(t) \, dt \geq \int_{z_2+1}^{x} f''(z_2 + 1) \, dt,$$

for $x \geq z_2 + 1$. The *Fundamental theorem of Calculus* tells us

$$f'(x) - f'(z_2 + 1) \geq (x - z_2 - 1)f''(z_2 + 1).$$

From here, it is easy to see that

$$f'(x) = f'(z_2 + 1) + (x - z_2 - 1)f''(z_2 + 1) \to \infty \quad \text{as} \quad x \to \infty.$$

So, f' is unbounded. Since f' starts negative, is decreasing on the interval $[0, z_2]$, and is increasing without bound on the interval $[z_2, \infty)$, f' has a unique zero, say z_1. We can prove f is unbounded using a nearly identical argument to the one we used to show f' is unbounded. Due to the fact that f starts out negative, is decreasing on the interval $[0, z_1]$, and is increasing without bound on the interval $[z_1, \infty)$, f has a unique zero.

Since I is false and II and III are true, we conclude that (D) is correct. ■

Question 3.56. ────────────────────────────────

For all of the counterexamples, assume $d : \mathbb{R}^2 \to \mathbb{R}$ is the Euclidian metric on $\mathbb{R}$, i.e. $d(x, y) := |x - y|$. A definition of a *metric* is located in the glossary.

The function $4 + d$ is not a metric, because the distance between a point and itself is not 0. Consider $(4+d)(1, 1) = 4+d(1, 1) = 4 \neq 0$.

The function $e^d - 1$ is not a metric, because the triangle inequality fails to hold. Consider the points $\log 3$, $\log 2$, and 0. Then $e^{d(\log 3, 0)} - 1 = 2$ but

$$e^{d(\log 3, \log 2)} - 1 + e^{d(\log 2, 0)} - 1 = \frac{3}{2} - 1 + 2 - 1 = \frac{3}{2} \not> 2$$

See the glossary if you have questions about the *logarithm properties* used.

The function $d - |d|$ is not a metric, because the distance between non-equal points is 0. For example, $(d - |d|)(1, 0) = 1 - 1 = 0$.

The function d^2 is not a metric, because it doesn't satisfy the triangle inequality criterion. Consider the points 1, $1/2$, and 0. Then

$$(d^2)(1, 0) = (1)^2 = 1$$

and

$$d^2 \left(1, \frac{1}{2}\right) + d^2 \left(\frac{1}{2}, 0\right) = \left(\frac{1}{2}\right)^2 + \left(\frac{1}{2}\right)^2 = \frac{1}{2} \not> 1.$$

By the processes of elimination $\sqrt{d}$ must be a metric and (E) is the correct answer, but let's prove it! Non-negativity and symmetry follow directly from d being a metric, which means all we need to prove is the triangle inequality. It's true that

$$\sqrt{x + y} \leq \sqrt{x} + \sqrt{y}$$

for x and y non-negative; to prove this, simply square both sides and cancel as needed. With this in mind, it follows that

$$\sqrt{d(x, y)} \leq \sqrt{d(x, z) + d(z, y)} \leq \sqrt{d(x, z)} + \sqrt{d(z, y)}.$$

∎

Question 3.57. ────────────────────────────────
See the glossary for a definition of a *ring*. Note that a subring U of a ring R is simply a ring such that $U \subseteq R$.

Set I is a subring, since the sum, difference, and product of polynomials with no linear term have no linear term. It's clear that both the additive identity of 0 and multiplicative identity 1 are still in our ring. The other criteria necessary for a ring clearly hold.

The set described by II is not a subring because it is not closed under addition. Both $x^2 + x$ and $-x^2$ have even degree, but

$$(x^2 + x) + (-x^2) = x$$

has odd degree.

Set III must be a subring. Since $\mathbb{Q}$ is a subfield of $\mathbb{R}$, there is no way for our third set to fail the axioms.

We pick (C), and continue! ■

Question 3.58. ────────────────────────────────
Property I is true. The set S is connected since the image of a connected set under a continuous map is connected.

The necessity of property II is debunked by $f(x) := 1$, because $S = \{f(c) : 0 < c < 1\} = \{1\}$ is not open.

Property III is true. The function f is continuous on all of $\mathbb{R}$. So, $S \subseteq f([0, 1])$, because $(0, 1) \subset [0, 1]$ and f is defined at 0 and 1. The set $f([0, 1])$ is *compact* because the image of a compact set under a continuous function is compact. Therefore, $f([0, 1])$ is bounded via an application of the *Heine-Borel theorem*. It follows that S is also bounded.

Option (C) is right because I and III are true and II is false. ■

Question 3.59.
The set $\{x^3, x^5, x^9\}$ has two distinct elements. That means
$$x^9 = x^3, \quad x^9 = x^5, \quad \text{or} \quad x^5 = x^3.$$

This implies
$$x^6 = 1, \quad x^4 = 1, \quad \text{or} \quad x^2 = 1,$$
where 1 is the identity element in our *group*.

Due to *Lagrange's theorem*, the order of a subgroup must divide the order of the group. However, 2 and 4 do not divide 15, which means if $x^4 = 1$ or $x^2 = 1$ were true $x = 1$ otherwise $\langle x \rangle$ would have order 2 or 4, an impossibility. But x cannot be 1 because it contradicts the fact that $\{x^3, x^5, x^9\}$ has two distinct elements. Thus,
$$x^6 = 1.$$

It follows that $\langle x \rangle$ has order 3 since 3 is the only common factor of 6 and 15 other than 1. Ergo,
$$\langle x^{13} \rangle = \{x^{13n} : n \text{ is a positive integer}\}$$

also has order 3, because 13 does not divide 15. Select (A). ■

Question 3.60.
Property I is legit. Consider the following argument:
$$s + s = (s + s)^2$$
$$= (s + s)(s + s)$$
$$= s^2 + s^2 + s^2 + s^2$$
$$= s + s + s + s.$$

Adding $-(s + s)$ to both sides yields the desired result.

Property II is valid; $(s + t)^2 = s + t = s^2 + t^2$.

Property III is also true. From property I, we know $s + s = 0$, which implies $s = -s$. Furthermore,
$$s + t = (s + t)^2$$
$$= s^2 + ts + st + t^2$$
$$= s + st + ts + t.$$

134

Adding $s + t$ to both sides gives us $st + ts = 0$. Hence, $st = -ts$. Because every element is its own additive inverse, we know $-ts = ts$. The result follows.

Since all of the properties are valid, we conclude (E) is correct. ■

Question 3.61. ────────────────────────────

The first step is to factor. It's clear

$$p^4 - 1 = (p-1)(p+1)(p^2+1).$$

Since p is a prime greater than 5, we can be confident that it is odd. Hence, both $p - 1$, $p + 1$, and $p^2 + 1$ are even. Furthermore, either $p - 1$ or $p + 1$ is divisible by 4, because every other even number is divisible by 4. It follows that $4 \cdot 2 \cdot 2 = 16$ divides $p^4 - 1$.

The numbers $p - 1$, p, and $p + 1$ are consecutive and, in a list of three consecutive numbers, one is always divisible by 3. Since p is a prime greater than 5, it cannot have 3 has a factor. It follows that either $p - 1$ or $p + 1$ is divisible by 3. So far we have $16 \cdot 3 = 48$ divides $p^4 - 1$.

Fermat's little theorem says

$$a^{q-1} \equiv 1 \pmod{q},$$

when q is a prime that does not divide a. It follows that

$$p^4 \equiv 1 \pmod 5,$$

or equivalently 5 divides $p^4 - 1$. Thus, $48 \cdot 5 = 240$ divides $p^4 - 1$.

We have not concluded that this is the largest number that divides $p^4 - 1$. However, 240 in choice (E) is our largest option, which is sufficient for the GRE. ■

135

Question 3.62. ───────────────────────────────
We could compute the third derivative and use *Taylor's theorem* to obtain the result, but finding the third derivative of $(1+x)^3(2+x^2)^{10}$ is computationally intensive. Instead, recall *Newton's binomial theorem*:

$$(x+y)^n = \sum_{k=0}^{n} \binom{n}{k} x^{n-k} y^k.$$

Thus,

$(1+x)^3(2+x^2)^{10}$

$$= \left(\binom{3}{0} + \binom{3}{1}x + \binom{3}{2}x^2 + \binom{3}{3}x^3 \right) \left(\binom{10}{0}2^{10} + \binom{10}{1}2^9 x^2 \right.$$
$$\left. + \ldots + \binom{10}{10}x^{20} \right)$$
$$= \left(1 + 3x + 3x^2 + x^3\right)\left(2^{10} + 10 \cdot 2^9 x^2 + 55 \cdot 2^8 x^4 + \ldots + x^{20}\right)$$

For polynomials $a_0 + a_1 x + \ldots + a_n x^n$ and $b_0 + b_1 x + \cdots + b_m x^m$, the product is

$$(a_0 + a_1 x + \ldots + a_n x^n)(b_0 + b_1 x + \cdots + b_m x^m) = \sum_{k=0}^{m+n} \left(\sum_{i+j=k} a_i b_j \right) x^k,$$

where $i = 0, 1, \ldots, n$ and $j = 0, 1, \ldots, m$. In particular, the coefficient in front of x^k is

$$\sum_{i+j=k} a_i b_j,$$

where $i = 0, 1, \ldots, n$ and $j = 0, 1, \ldots, m$.

Hence, the coefficient in front of x^3 will be

$$3 \cdot 10 \cdot 2^9 + 2^{10} = (30 + 2)\,2^9$$
$$= 2^5 \cdot 2^9$$
$$= 2^{14}.$$

Fill in the bubble for (A). ■

Question 3.63. ————————————————————————

Let's list the obvious first:

$$\lim_{x \to -\infty} x^{12} = \infty, \qquad 0^{12} = 0, \qquad \lim_{x \to \infty} x^{12} = \infty,$$

$$\lim_{x \to -\infty} 2^x = 0, \qquad 2^0 = 1, \qquad \lim_{x \to \infty} 2^x = \infty,$$

and

$$\lim_{x \to -\infty} 2^x - x^{12} = \infty.$$

Furthermore, we know 2^x increases monotonically for all x in $\mathbb{R}$, and x^{12} decreases monotonically when $x \le 0$ and increases monotonically when $x \ge 0$. So we can be confident that both graphs behave relatively well.

We're ready to make our conclusions:

It's clear the graph of x^{12} starts above the graph of 2^x because $x^{12} \to \infty$ as $x \to -\infty$ and $2^x \to 0$ as $x \to -\infty$. However, the graphs intersect for one value of x in $(-\infty, 0)$ because $2^0 = 1 > 0^{12} = 0$. There is only one such x in $(-\infty, 0)$ due to the monotonicity of both graphs.

There is another intersection on the interval $(0, 2)$, because 2^{12} is greater than 2^2. This is the only intersection because we know how both graphs more-or-less look on the interval $(0, 2)$.

Lastly, 2^x eventually gets bigger than x^{12}, so there must be one more intersection. This is the last intersection because 2^x grows faster than x^{12} when $2^x > x^{12}$ and x is positive.

It follows that there is a total of three points where the graphs intersection. As such, we select (D). ■

137

Question 3.64. ─────────────────────────────────

Property I is true. Since f is continuous, $f([0,1])$ is *compact*, and the *Heine-Borel theorem* tells us that this implies that it is closed and bounded. Hence,

$$M = \sup_{x \in [0,1]} \{f(x)\} \quad \text{and} \quad m = \inf_{x \in [0,1]} \{f(x)\},$$

for some m and M in $\mathbb{R}$. Let $C := M - m$.

Property II is also legitimate. Recall that if f has a compact domain, then its continuity implies it has *uniform continuity*. Thus, for all $\varepsilon > 0$, there exists a $\delta > 0$ such that $|x - y| < \delta$ implies $|f(x) - f(y)| < \varepsilon$. Pick $\varepsilon = 1$ and let D equal any δ that satisfies the uniform continuity criterion.

Property III is false. It's called "*Lipschitz continuity*", and claiming a function is Lipschitz continuous is a stronger statement about the function than continuity is. Let's find a function that is continuous on $[0, 1]$ but not Lipschitz continuous. To make our task a bit easier, notice that Lipschitz continuity is equivalent to saying there is a constant E such that

$$\left| \frac{f(x) - f(y)}{x - y} \right| \leq E$$

for all x and y in $[0, 1]$ and $x \neq y$. Consider $f(x) := \sqrt{x}$, which satisfies the assumptions of the question. We have

$$\left| \frac{f(x) - f(y)}{x - y} \right| = \left| \frac{\sqrt{x} - \sqrt{y}}{x - y} \right| = \left| \frac{1}{\sqrt{x} + \sqrt{y}} \right|$$

goes to infinity as x and y independently go to zero, so the ratio cannot be bounded.

Hence, (C) is right. ∎

Question 3.65. ————————————————————————

Suppose α_1, α_2, and α_3 are zeros of a third degree monic (i.e. the coefficient in front of x^3 is 1) polynomial q. Then

$$q(x) = (x - \alpha_1)(x - \alpha_2)(x - \alpha_3)$$
$$= x^3 - (\alpha_1 + \alpha_2 + \alpha_3)x^2 + (\alpha_1\alpha_2 + \alpha_1\alpha_3 + \alpha_2\alpha_3)x - \alpha_1\alpha_2\alpha_3.$$

Due to the remarks above, the three zeros must multiply to $-c$. Since -3 and 2 are zeros of p, the third zero must be $c/6$. It follows that
$$p(x) = (x + 3)(x - 2)\left(x - \frac{c}{6}\right).$$

This implies

$$p'(x) = (x - 2)\left(x - \frac{c}{6}\right) + (x + 3)\left(x - \frac{c}{6}\right) + (x + 3)(x - 2).$$

So,
$$p'(-3) = 15 + \frac{5c}{6} < 0.$$

Hence,
$$c < -18.$$

Only option (A) meets this criterion. ∎

Question 3.66. ───────────────────────────────────
Using *Green's theorem*, it follows that

$$\oint_C -2y\ dx + x^2\ dy = \iint\limits_{\{(x,y):\ x^2+y^2\le 9\}} \frac{\partial}{\partial x}\left(x^2\right) - \frac{\partial}{\partial y}\left(-2y\right)\ dA$$

$$= \iint\limits_{\{(x,y):\ x^2+y^2\le 9\}} 2x + 2\ dA$$

$$= \iint\limits_{\{(r,\theta):\ 0\le r\le 3,\ 0\le\theta\le 2\pi\}} \left(2r\cos\theta + 2\right)\ rdrd\theta$$

$$= \int_0^{2\pi}\int_0^3 2r^2\cos\theta + 2r\ drd\theta$$

$$= \int_0^{2\pi} 18\cos\theta + 9\ d\theta$$

$$= 18\pi.$$

Note: we switched to *polar coordinates* above, which required the following two formulae

$$x = r\cos\theta \qquad \text{and} \qquad dA = rdrd\theta.$$

Pick (E) and take a break! You earned it. ■

Glossary

Alternating series test Consider the infinite series $\sum a_n$ and suppose

$$a_n = (-1)^n b_n,$$

where b_n is positive and decreases monotonically. Then $\sum a_n$ converges if and only if

$$\lim_{n \to \infty} b_n = 0.$$

Antiderivatives Useful antiderivatives.

- $\displaystyle \int u^n \, du = \frac{u^{n+1}}{n+1} + C, \quad n \neq -1$

- $\displaystyle \int e^u \, du = e^u + C$

- $\displaystyle \int \frac{du}{u} = \log|u| + C$

- $\displaystyle \int \sin u \, du = -\cos u + C$

- $\displaystyle \int \cos u \, du = \sin u + C$

- $\displaystyle \int \tan u \, du = -\log|\cos u| + C$

- $\displaystyle \int \frac{du}{1+u^2} = \operatorname{Arctan} u + C$

Arc length

- The arc length of the curve from $x = a$ to $x = b$ described by $y = f(x)$ is

$$\int_a^b \sqrt{1 + \left(\frac{dy}{dt}\right)^2}\, dx.$$

- The arc length of the curve from $t = a$ to $t = b$ described by $(x, y) = \big(f(t), g(t)\big)$ is

$$\int_a^b \sqrt{\left(\frac{dx}{dt}\right)^2 + \left(\frac{dy}{dt}\right)^2}\, dt.$$

- The arc length of the curve from $\theta = \alpha$ to $\theta = \beta$ described by the polar equation $r = f(\theta)$ is

$$\int_\alpha^\beta \sqrt{r^2 + \left(\frac{dr}{d\theta}\right)^2}\, d\theta.$$

Basis The set $\mathcal{B}$ is a basis of a vector space V over a field $\mathbb{F}$ if and only if the following hold.

- The set $\mathcal{B}$ is nonempty.

- Every element in V can be written as a linear combination of elements in $\mathcal{B}$.

- The elements of $\mathcal{B}$ are linearly independent.

Binomial distribution Suppose n independent trials are conducted, each of which can either end in success or failure. Let p be the probability success. Then the probability of exactly k trials ending in success is

$$\binom{n}{k} p^k (1 - p)^{n-k}.$$

Furthermore, in a binomial distribution:

142

- The mean is $\mu = np$.

- The variance is $\sigma^2 = np(1-p)$.

- The standard deviation is $\sigma = \sqrt{np(1-p)}$.

Cardinal arithmetic Let A and B be sets.

- $|A| + |B| = |A \coprod B|$, where $A \coprod B$ denotes the disjoint union of A and B.

- $|A||B| = |A \times B|$.

- $\left|\{f \mid f : A \to B\}\right| = |B|^{|A|}$.

- $|A| \cdot |B| = \sup\{|A|, |B|\}$ if $|A|$ or $|B|$ is an infinite cardinal.

Cauchy's residue theorem Suppose U is a simply connected open subset of $\mathbb{C}$ and f is a function holomorphic on $U \setminus \{a_1, a_2, \ldots, a_n\}$. Let C be a positively oriented simple closed curve whose graph is contained in U, and suppose $a_1, a_2, \ldots, a_n$ are inside of C. Then

$$\int_C f(z)\, dz = 2\pi i \sum_{k=1}^n \operatorname{Res}(f, a_k),$$

where for a_k a pole of order m

$$\operatorname{Res}(f, a_k) = \frac{1}{(m-1)!} \lim_{z \to c} \frac{d^{m-1}}{dz^{m-1}}\left((z - a_k)^m f(z) \right).$$

http://en.wikipedia.org/wiki/Residue_Theorem

Compact Consider the set X under some topology. A collection $\mathcal{U}$ of open sets is said to be an "open cover" of X if and only if

$$X \subseteq \bigcup_{U \in \mathcal{U}} U.$$

The set X is compact if and only if every open cover $\mathcal{U}$ has a finite subcover $\{U_1, U_2, \ldots, U_n\} \subseteq \mathcal{U}$ such that

$$X \subseteq U_1 \cup U_2 \cup \ldots \cup U_n.$$

Dense Suppose A and B are subsets of a topological space X. We say A is dense in B if and only if $cl(A) = B$. In other words, every point of B is a limit point of A or an element of A.

Derivative rules Suppose that f and g are differentiable on some domain D. Assume c and n are constants.

- Constant rule:
$$\frac{d}{dx}(c) = 0.$$

- Constant multiple rule:
$$(c \cdot f)'(x) = c \cdot f'(x).$$

- Power rule:
$$\frac{d}{dx}(x^n) = nx^{n-1}.$$

- Sum and difference rules:
$$(f \pm g)'(x) = f'(x) \pm g'(x).$$

- Product rule:
$$(f \cdot g)'(x) = f(x)g'(x) + f'(x)g(x).$$

- Quotient Rule:
$$\left(\frac{f}{g}\right)'(x) = \frac{g(x)f'(x) - f(x)g'(x)}{\left(g(x)\right)^2},$$
where $g(x) \neq 0$.

- Chain rule:
$$(f \circ g)'(x) = f'(g(x)) g'(x).$$

Derivatives Useful derivatives.

$$\bullet \ \frac{d}{dx}u^n = nu^{n-1}u'$$

$$\bullet \ \frac{d}{dx}e^u = u'e^u$$

$$\bullet \ \frac{d}{dx}\log|u| = \frac{u'}{u}$$

$$\bullet \ \frac{d}{dx}\sin u = u'\cos u$$

$$\bullet \ \frac{d}{dx}\cos u = -u'\sin u$$

$$\bullet \ \frac{d}{dx}\tan u = u'\sec^2 u$$

$$\bullet \ \frac{d}{dx}\text{Arctan } u = \frac{u'}{1+u^2}$$

Derivatives have no "simple discontinuities" Suppose f is differentiable on the open interval (a,b) and c is in (a,b). Then

$$\lim_{x\to c^-} f'(x) = \lim_{x\to c^+} f'(x),$$

if both limits exist.

Descartes' rule of signs Suppose $f(x) = a_n x^n + a_{n-1}x^{n-1} + \ldots + a_1 x + a_0$. Then the number of positive zeros of f is equal to the number of sign changes of $f(x)$ or an even number fewer. Furthermore, the number of negative zeros of f is equal to the number of sign changes of $f(-x)$ or an even number fewer.

Determinant properties Suppose A and B are $n \times n$ matrices.

- The matrix A is invertible if and only if $\det(A) \neq 0$.
- If A^{-1} exists, $\det(A^{-1}) = 1/\det(A)$.
- For k in $\mathbb{R}$, $\det(kA) = k^n \det(A)$.
- The value of $\det(AB) = \det(A)\det(B)$.
- For k an integer, $\det(A^k) = \big(\det(A)\big)^k$.

Directional derivative Suppose all first order partial derivatives of f exist at the point P. Then the directional derivative of f in the direction of $\boldsymbol{u} \neq \boldsymbol{0}$ is

$$D_{\boldsymbol{u}}f\big|_P := \nabla f\big|_P \cdot \frac{\boldsymbol{u}}{|\boldsymbol{u}|},$$

where $\cdot$ denotes the dot product.

Discriminant Consider a quadratic function $f(x) = ax^2 + bx + c$, where a, b, and c are real and $a \neq 0$. The discriminant is $\Delta := b^2 - 4ac$.

- If $\Delta > 0$, f has two real zeros.

- If $\Delta = 0$, f has one real zero of multiplicity two.

- If $\Delta < 0$, f has two complex zeros.

Disk method Consider the solid generated by rotating the region between $y = k$ and $y = f(x)$ about $y = k$. Then its volume from $x = a$ to $x = b$ is

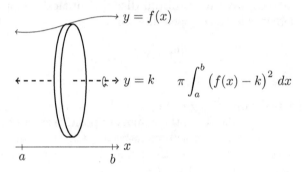

$$\pi \int_a^b \left(f(x) - k \right)^2 dx$$

The rotation about $x = h$ of the region between $x = h$ and $x = g(y)$ generates a three dimensional object. Its volume from $y = a$ to $y = b$ is

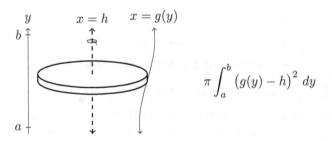

$$\pi \int_a^b \left(g(y) - h \right)^2 dy$$

Divergence theorem Suppose the closed surface S has outward orientation and is the boundary of a solid E, and $\boldsymbol{F}$ is a vector field with continuous first order partial derivatives. Then the flux of $\boldsymbol{F}$ through S is

$$\oiint_S \boldsymbol{F} \cdot d\boldsymbol{S} = \iiint_E \operatorname{div}(\boldsymbol{F}) \, dV,$$

where

$$\operatorname{div}(\boldsymbol{F}) := \left(\frac{\partial}{\partial x}, \frac{\partial}{\partial y}, \frac{\partial}{\partial z}\right) \cdot \boldsymbol{F}.$$

e

$$e := \sum_{k=0}^{\infty} \frac{1}{k!} = \lim_{n \to \infty} \left(\frac{n+1}{n}\right)^n.$$

Euler's formula $e^{i\theta} = \cos\theta + i\sin\theta$ for all θ in $\mathbb{C}$.

Extreme value theorem Let f be a continuous function from a compact set X to $\mathbb{R}$. Then there exist x_1 and x_2 in X such that

$$f(x_1) = \sup_{x \in X}\{f(x)\} \quad \text{and} \quad f(x_2) = \inf_{x \in X}\{f(x)\}.$$

Fermat's little theorem Suppose p is a prime number and a is an integer. Then

$$a^p \equiv a \pmod{p}.$$

If p does not divide a, then

$$a^{p-1} \equiv 1 \pmod{p}.$$

`http://en.wikipedia.org/wiki/Fermat's_little_theorem`

First derivative test Suppose $f : \mathbb{R} \to \mathbb{R}$ is continuous on the open interval (a, b) and differentiable on $(a, b) \setminus \{c\}$, where $a < c < b$.

- If $f'(x) > 0$ for x in (a, c) and $f'(x) < 0$ for x in (c, b), then $f(c)$ is a relative maximum.

- If $f'(x) < 0$ for x in (a, c) and $f'(x) > 0$ for x in (c, b), then $f(c)$ is a relative minimum.

147

In other words, if f' switches from positive to negative at c then $f(c)$ is a relative maximum, and if f' switches from negative to positive at c then $f(c)$ is a relative minimum.

Flux Let $\boldsymbol{F}$ be a vector field. Denote the flux of $\boldsymbol{F}$ through the surface S by Φ. We can calculate Φ by means of the limit of a Riemann sum. Consider the change in flux $\Delta\Phi$ which is the result of the flow of $\boldsymbol{F}$ through a small amount of the surface, say $\Delta\boldsymbol{S} := \boldsymbol{n}\Delta S$. We assume ΔS is small enough that it is approximately flat and $\boldsymbol{n}$ is a unit normal vector of ΔS. Then

$$\Delta\Phi \approx \boldsymbol{F} \cdot \Delta\boldsymbol{S} := \boldsymbol{F} \cdot \boldsymbol{n}\ \Delta S.$$

If θ is the acute angle between $\boldsymbol{F}$ and $\boldsymbol{n}$, then

$$\boldsymbol{F} \cdot \boldsymbol{n}\ \Delta S = |\boldsymbol{F}|\,|\boldsymbol{n}|\cos\theta\ \Delta S = |\boldsymbol{F}|\cos\theta\ \Delta S.$$

As our ΔS's become smaller and smaller,

$$\sum \Delta\Phi = \sum_{\Delta\boldsymbol{S}} \boldsymbol{F} \cdot \Delta\boldsymbol{S} = \sum_{\Delta\boldsymbol{S}} \boldsymbol{F} \cdot \boldsymbol{n}\ \Delta S \to \Phi$$

and

$$\sum_{\Delta\boldsymbol{S}} \boldsymbol{F} \cdot \Delta\boldsymbol{S} = \sum_{\Delta\boldsymbol{S}} \boldsymbol{F} \cdot \boldsymbol{n}\ \Delta S \to \oiint_S \boldsymbol{F} \cdot d\boldsymbol{S} = \oiint_S \boldsymbol{F} \cdot \boldsymbol{n}\ dS.$$

So,

$$\Phi = \oiint_S \boldsymbol{F} \cdot d\boldsymbol{S} = \oiint_S \boldsymbol{F} \cdot \boldsymbol{n}\ dS.$$

Note that in $\mathbb{R}^3$, at any point on a surface S there are always two unit normal vectors. The choice of which unit normal vector is used to describe S is called the "orientation" of S.

Let S be a subset of $\mathbb{R}^3$, and say $\boldsymbol{F}$ is a function of (x, y, z). Suppose $\boldsymbol{r}(u, v)$ is a parameterization of S, where (u, v) is in the set R. It can be shown that $d\boldsymbol{S} = \boldsymbol{r}_u \times \boldsymbol{r}_v\ dudv$, which implies

$$\oiint_S \boldsymbol{F}(x, y, z) \cdot d\boldsymbol{S} = \iint_R \boldsymbol{F}(\boldsymbol{r}) \cdot (\boldsymbol{r}_u \times \boldsymbol{r}_v)\ dudv.$$

When S is orientated upward and described by the equation $z = f(x, y)$, where (x, y) is in R, a popular parametrization of S is $\boldsymbol{r}(x, y) = \big(x, y, f(x, y)\big)$. This implies

$$\boldsymbol{r}_x \times \boldsymbol{r}_y = \big(-f_x(x, y), -f_y(x, y), 1\big).$$

Hence,

$$\oiint_S \boldsymbol{F}(x, y, z) \cdot d\boldsymbol{S}$$

$$= \iint_R \boldsymbol{F}\big(x, y, f(x, y)\big) \cdot \big(-f_x(x, y), -f_y(x, y), 1\big) \ dA.$$

Fundamental counting principle Suppose there are n_1 ways for an event to occur, and n_2 ways for another independent event to occur. Then there are

$$n_1 \cdot n_2$$

ways for the two events to occur. More generally, if there are n_i ways for the i-th independent event to occur, where $i = 1, 2, \ldots, m$, then there are

$$n_1 \cdot n_2 \cdot \ldots \cdot n_m$$

ways for the consecutive occurrence of the m events to occur.

Fundamental theorem of Calculus Suppose f is continuous on the closed interval $[a, b]$. Then

$$\int_a^b f(x) \ dx = F(b) - F(a),$$

where $F'(x) = f(x)$.

Fundamental theorem of finitely generated abelian groups Let G be a finitely generated abelian group. Then it is isomorphic to an expression of the form

$$\mathbb{Z}^k \times \mathbb{Z}_{p_1^{\alpha_1}} \times \mathbb{Z}_{p_2^{\alpha_2}} \times \ldots \mathbb{Z}_{p_n^{\alpha_m}},$$

where $k, \alpha_1, \alpha_2, \ldots, \alpha_m$ are whole numbers and $p_1, p_2, \ldots, p_m$ are primes which are not necessarily distinct. Alternatively, G is isomorphic to an expression of the form

$$\mathbb{Z}^k \times \mathbb{Z}_{r_1} \times \mathbb{Z}_{r_2} \times \ldots \times \mathbb{Z}_{r_n},$$

where $k, r_1, r_2, \ldots, r_n$ are whole numbers and r_i divides r_{i+1} for all $i = 1, 2, \ldots, n-1$. The values of k and each r_i are uniquely determined by G.

Green's theorem Let C be a piecewise smooth, simple closed curve in the xy-plane, which is oriented counterclockwise. Suppose D is the region bounded by C. Assume L and M are functions of x and y and have continuous partial derivatives on an open region containing D. Then

$$\oint_C L \, dx + M \, dy = \iint_D \frac{\partial M}{\partial x} - \frac{\partial L}{\partial y} \, dA.$$

http://en.wikipedia.org/wiki/Green_theorem

Group The set G together with a binary operation $\cdot$ is a group if and only if the following properties of G and $\cdot$ hold:

- Closed: a and b in G implies $a \cdot b$ in G.

- Associative: for all a, b, and c in G, we have $(a \cdot b) \cdot c = a \cdot (b \cdot c)$.

- Contains the identity element: there is an element e such that $e \cdot a = a \cdot e = a$ for all a in G.

- Contains inverse elements: for all a in G there is a^{-1} such that $a \cdot a^{-1} = a^{-1} \cdot a = e$.

http://en.wikipedia.org/wiki/Group_(mathematics)

Heine-Borel theorem For all positive integers n, a set in $\mathbb{R}^n$ is closed and bounded if and only if it is compact.

Ideal A left ideal I of a ring R is a subring such that for all r in R we have $rI \subseteq I$. The subring I is a right ideal if for all r in R, we have $Ir \subseteq I$. If both criteria are met, then we say that I is a two-sided ideal or simply an ideal.

Inclusion-exclusion principle For finite sets $U_1, U_2, \ldots, U_n$,

$$\left| \bigcup_{k=1}^{n} U_k \right| = \sum_{k=1}^{n} |U_k| - \sum_{1 \le k < \ell \le n} |U_k \cap U_\ell| + \sum_{1 \le k < \ell < m \le n} |U_k \cap U_\ell \cap U_m|$$
$$- \ldots + (-1)^{n-1} |U_1 \cap U_2 \cap \cdots \cap U_n|.$$

http://en.wikipedia.org/wiki/Inclusion-exclusion_principle

Inflection point Suppose f is a twice differentiable real-valued function on the set $(a, b) \setminus \{c\}$, where $a < c < b$. Then a point $(c, f(c))$ is an inflection point of the graph of f if and only if $f''(x) < 0$ for x in (a, c) and $f''(x) > 0$ for x in (c, b), or $f''(x) > 0$ for x in (a, c) and $f''(x) < 0$ for x in (c, b). In other words, $(c, f(c))$ is an inflection point if and only if f'' switches signs at c.

Integration by parts Suppose u and v are differentiable functions of x. Then

$$\int u \, dv = uv - \int v \, du.$$

Integration properties Suppose f and g are integrable real-valued functions over the closed interval $[a, b]$. Let α and β be in $\mathbb{R}$, and let c be in $[a, b]$. Then

- $\displaystyle\int_a^b \alpha f(x) + \beta g(x) \, dx = \alpha \int_a^b f(x) \, dx + \beta \int_a^b g(x) \, dx$

- $\displaystyle\int_a^b f(x) \, dx = - \int_b^a f(x) \, dx$

- $\displaystyle\int_a^b f(x) \, dx = \int_a^c f(x) \, dx + \int_c^b f(x) \, dx$

- $\displaystyle\int_c^c f(x) \, dx = 0$

- $\displaystyle\int_a^b f(x) \, dx \le \int_a^b g(x) \, dx$, whenever $f(x) \le g(x)$ for x in $[a, b]$

151

Intermediate value theorem Suppose f is a real-valued continuous function on the interval $[a, b]$. For each y between $f(a)$ and $f(b)$, there is a c in $[a, b]$ such that $f(c) = y$.

Inverse function theorem Suppose f is one-to-one and has a continuous derivative f' within some connected open neighborhood of $x = a$. Further, assume the graph of f within this neighborhood contains the point (a, b). Then

$$(f^{-1})'(b) = \frac{1}{f'(a)}.$$

Inverse of a 2×2 invertible matrix Suppose $A := \begin{pmatrix} a & b \\ c & d \end{pmatrix}$ is invertible. Then

$$A^{-1} = \frac{1}{ad - bc} \begin{pmatrix} d & -b \\ -c & a \end{pmatrix}.$$

L'Hôspital's rule Let f and g be functions differentiable on $(a, b) \setminus \{c\}$, and $g(x) \neq 0$ for all x in $(a, b) \setminus \{c\}$, where c is in (a, b). Assume

$$\lim_{x \to c} f(x) = \lim_{x \to c} g(x) = 0$$

or

$$\lim_{x \to c} f(x) = \lim_{x \to c} g(x) = \pm\infty.$$

Then

$$\lim_{x \to c} \frac{f(x)}{g(x)} = \lim_{x \to c} \frac{f'(x)}{g'(x)}.$$

Lagrange's theorem Suppose G is a finite group and H is a subgroup of G. Then the order of H divides the order of G.

Law of cosines Consider $\triangle ABC$ shown below.

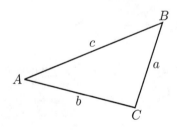

- $a^2 = b^2 + c^2 - 2bc \cos A$

- $b^2 = a^2 + c^2 - 2ac \cos B$

- $c^2 = a^2 + b^2 - 2ab \cos C$

Least upper bound The value x is the least upper bound of a set A if and only if the following criteria are satisfied:

- $x \geq a$ for all a in A,

- $y \geq a$ for all a in A implies $y \geq x$.

Lipschitz continuity Let (X, ρ) and (Y, σ) be metric spaces. A function $f : X \to Y$ is Lipschitz continuous if and only if there exists a real constant $C \geq 0$ such that for x_1 and x_2 in X,

$$\sigma\big(f(x_1), f(x_2)\big) \leq C\rho(x_1, x_2).$$

http://en.wikipedia.org/wiki/Lipschitz_continuity

Logarithm properties The GRE assumes log is base e <u>not</u> base 10.

- $\displaystyle\int \frac{du}{u} = \log|u| + C$

- $\log x = y \iff e^y = x$

- $\log(e^x) = x$ and $e^{\log x} = x$

- $\log 1 = 0$

- $\log e = 1$

- $\log(xy) = \log x + \log y$

- $\log\left(\dfrac{x}{y}\right) = \log x - \log y$

- $\log x^y = y \log x$

Maclaurin series formula Suppose the n-th derivative of f exists and is continuous. The Maclaurin polynomial of degree n for f is

$$\sum_{k=0}^{n} \frac{f^{(k)}(0)}{k!} x^k.$$

If f is infinitely differentiable, then

$$f(x) = \sum_{k=0}^{\infty} \frac{f^{(k)}(0)}{k!} x^k.$$

Well known Maclaurin series include:

- $e^x = \displaystyle\sum_{k=0}^{\infty} \frac{x^k}{k!}$

- $\cos x = \displaystyle\sum_{k=0}^{\infty} \frac{(-1)^k x^{2k}}{(2k)!}$

- $\sin x = \displaystyle\sum_{k=0}^{\infty} \frac{(-1)^k x^{2k+1}}{(2k+1)!}$

- $\dfrac{1}{1-x} = \displaystyle\sum_{k=0}^{\infty} x^k$, where $-1 < x < 1$

Mean value theorem Suppose f is continuous on the closed interval $[a, b]$ and differentiable on the open interval (a, b). Then there is some c in (a, b) such that

$$f'(c) = \frac{f(b) - f(a)}{b - a}.$$

Method of Lagrange multipliers Suppose $f(x, y, z)$ and $g(x, y, z)$ have continuous first order partial derivatives, and there is a constant k such that $g(x, y, z) = k$. Then relative extrema of f occur at points (x, y, z) that satisfy

$$f_x(x, y, x) = \lambda g_x(x, y, z), \qquad f_y(x, y, z) = \lambda g_y(x, y, z),$$
$$\text{and} \quad f_z(x, y, z) = \lambda g_z(x, y, z)$$

for some λ in $\mathbb{R}$.

Metric A metric on a set X is a function $d : X \times X \to \mathbb{R}$ such that for all x, y, and z in X the following criteria hold:

- Non-negativity: $d(x, y) \geq 0$ and $d(x, y) = 0$ if and only if $x = y$

- Symmetry: $d(x, y) = d(y, x)$

- Triangle inequality: $d(x, z) \leq d(x, y) + d(y, z)$.

Necessary and sufficient condition for a function to be analytic
The function $f(x + iy) = u(x, y) + iv(x, y)$ is analytic if and only if

$$\frac{\partial u}{\partial x} = \frac{\partial v}{\partial y} \quad \text{and} \quad \frac{\partial u}{\partial y} = -\frac{\partial v}{\partial x}.$$

Newton's binomial theorem

$$(x + y)^n = \sum_{k=0}^{n} \binom{n}{k} x^{n-k} y^k.$$

Partial fraction decomposition Suppose we have a rational expression of the form $p(x)/q(x)$ where p and q are polynomials with no common factors, the degree of q is larger than the degree of p, and $q \neq 0$. The objective of partial fraction decomposition is to write our rational expression as the sum of more simple rational expressions. What follows is a non-exhaustive list of rules:

Factor of q	Term(s) of partial fraction decomposition
$ax + b$	$\dfrac{A}{ax + b}$
$(ax + b)^m$	$\dfrac{A_1}{ax + b} + \dfrac{A_2}{(ax + b)^2} + \ldots + \dfrac{A_m}{(ax + b)^m}$
$ax^2 + bx + c$	$\dfrac{Ax + B}{ax^2 + bx + c}$
$(ax^2 + bx + c)^m$	$\dfrac{A_1 x + B_1}{ax^2 + bx + c} + \dfrac{A_2 x + B_2}{(ax^2 + bx + c)^2}$ $+ \ldots + \dfrac{A_m x + B_m}{(ax^2 + bx + c)^m},$

where $a, b, c, A, B, A_i,$ and B_i are real numbers, $a \neq 0$, and m is a natural number. For further explanation, we suggest any quality Calculus text, e.g. *Calculus* by Stewart.

Pigeonhole principle Suppose we want to put n items into m slots. Then there must be at least one slot that contains at least $\lceil n/m \rceil$ items and there must be a slot that holds no more than $\lfloor n/m \rfloor$.

Polar coordinates The following is a list of conversions between polar and rectangular coordinates.

$$x = r\cos\theta, \quad y = r\sin\theta, \quad r^2 = x^2 + y^2, \quad \text{and} \quad dA = rdrd\theta.$$

Probability properties Let X be the sample space, and A and B be events in X.

- $P(X) = 1$
- $P(\varnothing) = 0$
- $0 \le P(A) \le 1$
- $P(X \setminus A) = 1 - P(A)$
- $P(B) \le P(A)$ if $B \subseteq A$
- $P(A \setminus B) = P(A) - P(A \cap B)$
- $P(A \cup B) = P(A) + P(B) - P(A \cap B)$
- $P(A \cap B) = P(A) \cdot P(B)$ if A and B are independent events

Pythagorean identities Suppose θ is in $\mathbb{R}$. Then

$$\cos^2\theta + \sin^2\theta = 1, \quad 1+\tan^2\theta = \sec^2\theta, \quad \text{and} \quad 1+\cot^2\theta = \csc^2\theta.$$

Rank-nullity theorem Suppose V is a finite dimensional vector space and let $T : V \to W$ be a linear map. Then

$$\text{nullity}(T) + \text{rank}(T) = \dim(V)$$

Ratio test Consider the series $S := \sum_{n=1}^{\infty} a_n$ and the limit $L := \lim_{n\to\infty} \left| \dfrac{a_{n+1}}{a_n} \right|$.

- If $L < 1$ then S converges absolutely.
- If $L > 1$ then S does not converge.

- If $L = 1$ or L doesn't exist, then the test is inconclusive.

Rational roots theorem Suppose $p(x) = a_n x^n + a_{n-1} x^{n-1} + \ldots + a_0$ is a polynomial such that $a_1, a_2, \ldots, a_n$ are integers. Then every rational root can be reduced to p/q, where p is an integer factor of a_0 and q is an integer factor of a_n.

Ring A set R is a ring if and only if it is an abelian (commutative) group under $+$ and the following properties of R and $\cdot$ hold

- Associativity: $(a \cdot b) \cdot c = a \cdot (b \cdot c)$ for all a, b, and c in R.

- Distributive on the right: $a \cdot (b + c) = a \cdot b + a \cdot c$ for all a, b, and c in R.

- Distributive on the left: $(b + c) \cdot a = b \cdot a + c \cdot a$ for all a, b, and c in R.

http://en.wikipedia.org/wiki/Ring_(mathematics)

Schröder-Berstein theorem For A and B sets, $|A| \leq |B|$ and $|B| \leq |A|$ implies $|A| = |B|$.

Second derivatives test Suppose that the function $f : \mathbb{R}^2 \to \mathbb{R}$ has continuous second order partial derivatives in some $E \subseteq \mathbb{R}^2$. Suppose the point (a, b) in E is a critical point, i.e. $f_x(a, b) = 0$ and $f_y(a, b) = 0$. Define

$$H_f(x, y) := \det \begin{pmatrix} f_{xx}(x, y) & f_{xy}(x, y) \\ f_{yx}(x, y) & f_{yy}(x, y) \end{pmatrix}$$
$$= f_{xx}(x, y) f_{yy}(x, y) - (f_{xy}(x, y))^2.$$

- If $f_{xx}(a, b) > 0$ and $H_f(a, b) > 0$, then $f(a, b)$ is a relative minimum.

- If $f_{xx}(a, b) < 0$ and $H_f(a, b) > 0$, then $f(a, b)$ is a relative maximum.

- If $H_f(a, b) < 0$, then (a, b) is a saddle point.

- If $H_f(a, b) = 0$, then the test gives no information.

http://en.wikipedia.org/wiki/Second_partial_derivative_test

Sine and cosine values in quadrant I To convert the radian measures in the first row to degrees, simply multiply $180°/\pi$.

θ	0	$\pi/6$	$\pi/4$	$\pi/3$	$\pi/2$
$\cos\theta$	1	$\sqrt{3}/2$	$\sqrt{2}/2$	$1/2$	0
$\sin\theta$	0	$1/2$	$\sqrt{2}/2$	$\sqrt{3}/2$	1

Slope and concavity of curves with parametric equations
Suppose $x = f(t)$ and $y = g(t)$ are twice differentiable real-valued functions and t is a real number. At the point corresponding to t, the slope of the curve described by $\{(x(t), y(t)) \in \mathbb{R}^2 : t \text{ real}\}$ is

$$\frac{dy}{dx} = \frac{dy/dt}{dx/dt},$$

when $dx/dt \neq 0$. Furthermore, at the point corresponding to t, the concavity of the curve $\{(x(t), y(t)) \in \mathbb{R}^2 : t \text{ real}\}$ is

$$\frac{d^2y}{dx^2} = \frac{d^2y/dtdx}{dx/dt},$$

where $dx/dt \neq 0$.

Summation formulas

- $\displaystyle\sum_{k=1}^{n} a_k + b_k = \sum_{k=1}^{n} a_k + \sum_{k=1}^{n} b_k$

- $\displaystyle\sum_{k=1}^{n} c \cdot a_k = c \sum_{k=1}^{n} a_k$

- $\displaystyle\sum_{k=1}^{n} 1 = n$

- $\displaystyle\sum_{k=1}^{n} k = \frac{n(n+1)}{2}$

- $\displaystyle\sum_{k=1}^{n} k^2 = \frac{n(n+1)(2n+1)}{6}$

- $$\sum_{k=1}^{n} k^3 = \frac{n^2(n+1)^2}{4}$$

- $$\sum_{k=1}^{n} a_k = \frac{n(a_1 + a_n)}{2}, \text{ where } \sum a_k \text{ is an arithmetic series}$$

- $$\sum_{k=1}^{n} a_1 r^{k-1} = \frac{a_1(1 - r^n)}{1 - r}, \text{ where } r \neq 1$$

- $$\sum_{k=1}^{\infty} a_1 r^{k-1} = \frac{a_1}{1 - r}, \text{ where } |r| < 1$$

Taylor's theorem Let f be a real-valued function defined on some set which contains the interval $[a, b]$. Suppose $f^{(n)}$ is continuous on $[a, b]$ and $f^{(n+1)}$ exists on the open interval (a, b), where n is a positive integer. Then for each x and c in $[a, b]$ there is a z between x and c such that

$$f(x) = \frac{f^{(n+1)}(z)}{(n + 1)!}(x - c)^{n+1} + \sum_{k=0}^{n} \frac{f^{(k)}(c)}{k!}(x - c)^k.$$

Hence, f can be approximated by the polynomial

$$\sum_{k=0}^{n} \frac{f^{(k)}(c)}{k!}(x - c)^k,$$

and the error is less than or equal to the Lagrange error bound of

$$\frac{\sup_{z \in I} |f^{(n+1)}(z)|}{(n + 1)!}|x - c|^{n+1},$$

where I is the open interval with endpoints x and c.

Uniform continuity Consider the metric spaces (X, ρ) and (Y, σ). A function $f : X \to Y$ is uniformly continuous on $U \subseteq X$ if and only if for all $\varepsilon > 0$ there is a $\delta > 0$ such that

$$\sigma\big(f(x_1), f(x_2)\big) < \varepsilon \quad \text{whenever} \quad \rho(x_1, x_2) < \delta,$$

for all x_1 and x_2 in U.

Uniform convergence theorem Suppose $\{f_n\}_{n=1}^{\infty}$ is a sequence of continuous functions that converge point-wise to the function f. If $\{f_n\}_{n=1}^{\infty}$ converges uniformly to f on an interval S, then f is continuous on S. See `http://en.wikipedia.org/wiki/Uniform_convergence`.

Washer method Consider the region bound between $y = f(x)$ and $y = g(x)$, where $f(x) \geq g(x)$ for x in the interval $[a, b]$. Then the volume of the solid from $x = a$ to $x = b$ generated by revolving the region about the x-axis is

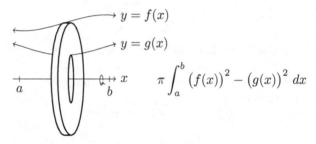

$$\pi \int_a^b \left(f(x)\right)^2 - \left(g(x)\right)^2 \, dx$$

Consider the region bound between $x = f(y)$ and $x = g(y)$, where $f(y) \geq g(y)$ for y in the interval $[a, b]$. Then the volume of the solid from $y = a$ to $y = b$ generated by revolving the region about the y-axis is

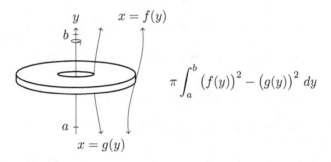

$$\pi \int_a^b \left(f(y)\right)^2 - \left(g(y)\right)^2 \, dy$$

Work Let $C := \{\gamma(t) : a \leq t \leq b\}$, where $\gamma : \mathbb{R} \to \mathbb{R}^n$ is differentiable in each coordinate. Then the work done by a vector field $\boldsymbol{F}$ over C is

$$W = \int_C \boldsymbol{F} \cdot d\gamma = \int_a^b \boldsymbol{F} \cdot \gamma'(t) \, dt.$$

CPSIA information can be obtained
at www.ICGtesting.com
Printed in the USA
FSHW02n0833120818
51365FS